# ENDORSEMENTS

I have had the privilege of knowing Wes Willmer for many many years and the opportunity to work alongside him, as we both are passionate about helping Christians understand and use money in the way that God intended. Scripture is certainly full of biblical wisdom principles when it comes to money and money management. I have for many years taught something called the paradox of prosperity which is very simply the more stuff you have the more difficult life becomes. You now have more and more choices to make. Poverty is not the answer to that paradox but faith is. How we view money is certainly a matter that greatly affects our souls. Thanks to Wes for writing this book. It will be another of his major contributions to the faith.

—RON BLUE, entrepreneur, author, and speaker

Jesus Christ wants us to be liberated from the greed for money that ultimately entangles and enslaves us, leading us to commit the sin of idolatry. For the past forty years, the Holy Spirit has been employing Wes Willmer powerfully to give true freedom to those who humbly submit themselves to the principle of stewardship and the cause of the Kingdom. This book is a must-read for all Christians who are striving to materialize the Kingdom values in their daily lives.

—SUNG WOOK CHUNG, Ph.D., Professor of Christian Theology, Denver Seminary, and President, Kurios International

Well before he and I served together, I knew of Wes Willmer and his significant contribution to the church on issues of biblical generosity and stewardship. His ability to write with mind and heart— intellectually and spiritually— on matters of importance to Christians has always been a characteristic of Wes and appreciated by many. I believe you'll find this to be true of *Stuff and Soul* as well.

—BARRY H. COREY, Ph.D., President of Biola University and author of *Love Kindness: Discover the Power of a Forgotten Christian Virtue*

God placed us in charge of the Earth and its contents. As believers of Christ, we must recognize our steward responsibilities by relying on the Holy Spirit to posture our hearts to live generously. In this book, Willmer (and Hogan) demonstrate this point and provide practical application of what this means personally, in the raising of children, and in the faithful overseeing of churches. As explained, giving generously of time, talents, and treasure is a spiritual discipline that allows us to know God and His goodness more fully. This book outlines the integral nature of our soul and the stuff God provides for us. This is not a taboo topic to avoid in the church, but rather a necessary discipleship opportunity in the spiritual maturing of believers.

—JOHN C. VAN DRUNEN, Executive Pastor, Fellowship Bible Church

I enthusiastically recommend Wes's book, *Stuff and Soul: Mastering the Critical Connection.* I have known Wes for over twenty years and have benefited greatly from his biblical wisdom and how it applies to my daily life. As the title suggests, this book points to the important role our possessions, and how we relate to them, play in influencing our spiritual journey. For me, this book is a critical reminder of what truly matters in life.

—TODD HARPER, President, Generous Giving

Wes Willmer adjusts your vision so you can fully see and understand God's true intention for being and doing. He reconstructs the significance between who you are and the stuff that fills your lives. Refreshing and challenging, this book reframed my thinking and how I am living. Don't miss this chance to nurture and inspire your soul!

—TAMI HEIM, President and CEO, Christian Leadership Alliance

This book explores the relationship between the soul and stuff with a rare combination of spiritual depth and practical usefulness. Souls discover that when we handle stuff according to the teachings of Scripture, it shapes much more than just our giving. The process transforms our affections and relationships so that we grasp life in the present and rewards in eternity. I found Willmer's keys to mastery especially helpful for applying the biblical wisdom he sets forth.

—GARY G. HOAG, Ph.D., President/CEO, Global Trust Partners

Once again, Wes Willmer takes every believer to the heart of the matter in his latest book, *Stuff and Soul*. His clarion call in this book champions a gospel-centered approach to life, living and giving so you can someday hear, "Well done, good and faithful servant! You have been faithful with a few things; I will put you in charge of many things. Come and share your master's happiness!"

—BRIAN KLUTH, speaker and author of the *40 Day Spiritual Journey to a More Generous Life* devotional

Jesus said, "For where your treasure is, there your heart will be also" (Matt 6:21). Tragically, many American Christians have allowed earthly treasure, or the pursuit of such, to capture and consume their hearts. This obsession with wealth and possessions has caused the church to become lethargic. It's been aptly said, "Prosperity has often been fatal to Christianity, but persecution never." Indeed, the debilitating weakness of the church is prosperity . . . and the comfort it brings. In *Stuff and Soul*, Dr. Willmer challenges Christians to be wise and sacrificial stewards who understand how to invest their time, talents, and treasure in light of eternity. Willmer's writing is inspiring and challenging. Most importantly, *Stuff and Soul* will move you to obey Jesus' command: "Do not store up for yourselves treasures on earth . . . But store up for yourselves treasures in heaven" (Matt 6:19a, 20a).

—KEITH R. KRELL, Ph.D., DMin., Senior Pastor, Crossroads Bible Church, Bellevue, WA., co-author of *Paul and Money*

It's true. The world is stuffocated. We buy houses with three-car garages, fill them with stuff, park our cars outside, and buy a storage unit for more of our stuff. When I first read God and Your Stuff in 2002, my garage was overflowing with bins of stuff. Today, the book is marked up, dog-eared, highlighted, paperclipped, and tattered. My garage on the other hand has room for bikes and tools and has a whole lot less junk. I noticed that in the margin of the book on one page, I jotted down, "Wow! This is ME!" Wes had written, "Give all you can," and since then we've set out to do just that. Wes is an icon in this biblical stewardship space, and I've used Wes's writing for teaching, for my own thinking, and I've shared it with others. Its message has deeply penetrated my life and the lives of those I have shared its principles with. This current book, *Stuff and Soul*, takes me even deeper in understanding the critical connection between my stuff and my soul's spiritual health. Get your copy and your garage will have more space!

—GREG LEITH, CEO, Convene Inc.

Life isn't simple! It is complicated and turns into a huge maintenance job over time. Why? Because as we go through life we accumulate "Stuff." "Stuff" is property, things that were important 5 years ago-but less so now, relationships, and money—anything that requires time and attention. So how do we deal with all the "Stuff?" More importantly how does God view our "Stuff?" How does God want us to manage what has been entrusted into our care during this physical life? Wes Willmer has been helping people deal with these critical issues for years! He applies biblical principles to life situations we deal with every day. Join Wes, as he outlines a roadmap to uncomplicate our harried, fragmented, "stuff-centered" lives. Every family should read and absorb these biblical, common sense, principles. Why? Because they have helped the Libby family untangle life! Start untangling yours today!

—LAUREN LIBBY, International President and CEO,
TWR International

Early in my career as a fundraiser for Asian Theological Seminary, Wes Willmer was my mentor without him knowing it! His books tutored me in Christian fundraising. He is aptly called the patriarch and pioneer in this area. His books are classics. The truths in the topics discussed transcend cultures, denominational, and theological boundaries. *Stuff and Soul* is a must-read book for all Christians, especially those in the business of giving and receiving.

—ZENET MARAMARA, DMin, faculty, Asian Theological Seminary,
Manila, Philippines; President, Christian Stewardship Association
and founder of the Fundraising Institute

Wes has been a pioneer for the cause of Biblical stewardship and a Christ-centered understanding of our relationship to the material things God entrusts to us. Building on his thoughtful work in *God and Your Stuff,* Wes now challenges us to go deeper by making the unequivocal link between our relationship to our stuff and the state of our soul. *Stuff and Soul* is an uncompromising, yet winsome invitation to examine our hearts and attitudes regarding the things of this world. There is no agenda of guilt here, but a discovery of the freedom that only comes from the surrendered heart of a faithful steward. Take the journey, and see if God does not use Wes' words to set you free to cultivate a right relationship between your stuff and your soul.

—R. Scott Rodin, Ph.D., President, The Steward's Journey

Having served as a local church pastor for decades, my experience is that one of the greatest voids in the church today among pastors, board members, treasurers, and other lay leaders is a biblical understanding and practice of biblical financial stewardship. I have found in our church that books written by Wes Willmer are excellent resources and we have used them in many ways to fill this void among our staff and congregation. I would readily recommend *Stuff and Soul* for use in any church body.

—Dr. Gary Stewart, Senior Pastor, Beaverdam Baptist Church

What Wes Willmer writes, thoughtful people want to read. Grateful that Wes is still helping us navigate the rough waters of material seduction and keeping us on track toward the hefty ROI of Kingdom investment!

—Joseph M. Stowell, Ph.D., President, Cornerstone University

*Stuff and Soul* is a provocative book. It made me squirm a bit as I examined my own motives and practices of giving. Wes (Willmer) does not chide us to give more, but intellectually, scripturally and practically gives insight on what to think and do about money and our stuff. One thing is certain: discipleship without stewardship is empty. Releasing our death grip on our resources and possessions produces a profound personal freedom and an inexplicable joy. The connection to the life of our soul sheds new light on spiritual growth. This is a classic.

—JERRY E. WHITE, Ph.D., International President Emeritus,
The Navigators

*Stuff and Soul* is an excellent, transformative and much needed resource for pastors and church attenders to fill the void in understanding the vital link between their stuff and soul. If pastors will communicate these truths to their churches and Christians will master this key connection of the *Stuff and Soul*, God's eternal kingdom will be significantly advanced.

—CHRIS WILLARD, Leadership Network Director of Generosity
Initiatives, Generis Senior Generosity Strategist and co-author of
*Contagious Generosity: Creating a Culture of Giving in Your Church*

Wes Willmer is a nationally respected and influential thought leader in helping Christians integrate their faith in Christ with their possessions and encouraging believers to be generous as Christ is generous. He has actively studied and taught about God and money, God and giving and God and asking. In *Stuff and Soul*, he explains so clearly how there is an important eternal connection between earthly possessions (stuff) and our eternal soul. This book is both scholarly and practical and if all believers were to apply these practical principles it would radically change the Church today. This is a book that I will not just read, but one that I will use to deepen my faith and ministry potential. I highly recommend *Stuff and Soul* to all followers of Christ that desire to be more like Christ.

—DAVID WILLS, President Emeritus,
National Christian Foundation (USA)

This book will transform your life as you learn how to understand the dichotomy of the world's view of possessions and that of a biblical perspective. My prayer is that everyone will read this book and master the critical connection between stuff and soul.

—SID YEOMAN, President, Good $ense Movement

Complete
with a personal/
group study guide

# STUFF

# &

# Soul

## MASTERING THE CRITICAL CONNECTION

Wesley K. Willmer
*with* Micah Hogan

KINGDOM LIFE PUBLISHING

Requests for permissions should be addressed to:
Kingdom Life Publishing
P.O. Box 389
Colbert, WA 99005
U.S.A.

To contact the authors, email:
Wes.Willmer@gmail.com

Interior design and typeset by Katherine Lloyd, The DESK

ISBN 978-0-578-54884-5

Printed in the United States of America

# CONTENTS

# FOREWORD

C hristians struggle with connecting what they hear on Sunday to what they do on Monday and with the relationship of time to eternity, as well as with the meanings of work, wealth, possessions, and stewardship. We do so because we tend to compartmentalize aspects of our lives and thus divorce what we do with our stuff from the spiritual life of our souls. We struggle with compartmentalization because this is the way the culture tells us to live, relegating soul formation to one day of the week that rarely touches on how we use stuff the other six days of the week. Not only is this the way the world models for us, but it is also the way that sin influences us. We do not need a great excuse to continue using our stuff merely in the ways we see fit.

In this concise, well-written, and theologically sound book that you hold in your hands, Wes Willmer and Micah Hogan offer a wise course for Christian disciples to follow, proposing for us a holistic approach to life that integrates how we use our stuff with the shaping of our souls. The book is more than a book about giving, stewardship, or prioritizing life and possessions, though it certainly addresses all these things in a faithful manner. This volume provides a larger framework, a Christian world and life view, that allows believers to think biblically about today and tomorrow, and about how we live, think, and serve with our stuff in light of eternity. It shows us how to master this critical connection of stuff and soul.

It quickly becomes apparent that when we do not give God control of our possessions, they gain control of us. Both affluence and poverty lead to strain, anxiety, and sleeplessness. Everyone—rich, poor, or in between—needs guidance in what it means to use their stuff to form their soul in light of eternity. Willmer and Hogan provide this needful instruction for us, encouraging readers to love and enjoy God above all else in order to live faithfully and abundantly in Christ, using stuff to His glory and our own good. This encouragement is not hedonistic, nor materialistic, but is a reminder that all we have is from God. All of God's gifts to and for His people are good (James 1:17), which means they are not to be rejected or despised, but greatly appreciated and wisely stewarded, and this wisdom lies in learning to receive these things with gratitude.

As the first-century Christian teaching manual the Didache instructs believers then and now, we must choose between two ways of life. We can follow the world's model and our own sinful inclinations, which may result in ever-so-brief momentary pleasure, while never truly satisfying or providing ultimate security. Often the end results in disaster. Or we can heed the message echoed over and over throughout Scripture. We can, by God's Spirit, choose to live a life rich toward Him that forms our soul to experience His presence. We can build a life that begins and ends each day in thanksgiving to God for the blessings, privileges, opportunities, and responsibilities that come our way as gifts from God's good and gracious hand. Instead of pursuing our own agenda, Wes Willmer and Micah Hogan have outlined for us a way to enjoy God's goodness to us and to live as faithful stewards each day in light of God's providential and eternal plan. In doing so, we can live a life of sanctification that directs our souls toward God, one in which we can experience authentic and satisfying contentment, significance, security, and joy in our homes, in our work, in our churches, and in our communities, with family and with friends. We can find purpose and direction in life, as well as teaching regarding forgiveness and salvation, discipleship, and stewardship, which allow us to live lives of worship and adoration in the very presence of God. May God help us all to master this critical connection of stuff and soul so that we live lives that train our souls to hope in the Lord, from this time forth and forevermore.

—David S. Dockery, Ph.D.
Chancellor, Trinity International University/Trinity Evangelical Divinity School; President, Evangelical Theological Society

# PREFACE

I have been blessed by the wisdom of Wes Willmer over the years and am so grateful for all that I have learned from him. Wes has served on the Christian Leadership Alliance National Board of Directors and Advisory Council. He is one of the significant thought leaders in the areas of Christian leadership, particularly as he focuses on the challenges to Christian disciples in the area of faith and finances.

Wes is considered an icon on this topic, as he has been a pioneer among recent Christian leaders in encouraging fellow believers through his writing and speaking to follow God's plan for money, giving, and asking. Frequently in the Christian Leadership Alliance's *Outcomes* magazine (and other publications), authors acknowledge how the previous writings and speaking of Wes have impacted their lives and work. Leaders frequently cite his work as a framework for their opinions.

One of the greatest challenges Christian disciples must face in today's culture is how the use of possessions impacts us spiritually. The scholar and theologian John Stott notes that "A preoccupation with material things can smother our spiritual life." How true! And for this reason, I am delighted that Wes Willmer has provided this book to help us master the critical connection between stuff and soul. This short book provides a biblical and theologically sound practical direction for all of us to follow. It instructs individuals and explains the role of the church on how to master this topic of stuff and soul.

As I interact with many church and parachurch leaders around the world, frequently they express how faith and finance issues are at the forefront of their concerns. This book will assist immensely in providing a guide to understand why Scripture has more verses on possessions than any other topic. You will begin to understand and master the vital link between the earthly possessions God entrusts us with and our eternal soul. As Wes points out, this is a critical connection and one we all need to master.

This book is written to help you and me. It is biblical, precise, and practical. I encourage you to read it, answer the mastery questions throughout, and use it in small groups by engaging with the study guide.

If Christians today were to adjust their lives to the principles in this book, they would be blessed by being rich toward God, and God's eternal Kingdom would be furthered. Will you join me today in mastering the critical connection between stuff and soul?

—Tami Heim
President and CEO, Christian Leadership Alliance

# INTRODUCTION

---

*Therefore, if anyone is in Christ, the new creation has come:*
*The old has gone, the new is here!*
—2 Corinthians 5:17

M ost of our lives are spent swimming in stuff—you could say we are "stuffocated"![1] Stuff comprises all the material resources around us, most specifically money and possessions. But here's the thing: God owns it all. The things that surround you every day—from your house to your car to the pennies in your couch cushions—belong to Him. In Psalm 24:1, the Psalmist declares:

"The earth *is* the Lord's, and all its fullness,
The world and those who dwell therein."

God is the Lord of all and He owns it all. Everything we have is really just on loan to us; "our" things aren't really ours at all, they are God's.

The reason God entrusts us with His things in this world is so that we can be "faithful stewards of God's grace in its various forms" (1 Pet. 4:10). A steward is someone who uses his or her master's things in the master's place to do the master's work. When Jesus ascended into heaven, He left His followers with the critical responsibility to be stewards of His resources in order to do His work. Stewarding His possessions for His glory is part of what it means to be His followers.

1

This means that every purchase, every allocation of funds, happens *coram Deo*, before God, and we will have to render an account for how we have used our Master's things. Every possession comes with a question: "how will you use me?" One day, we will be judged for our consumption of stuff, and will have to render an account to God. However, if we steward God's stuff according to His Spirit and according to His will, we will receive heavenly rewards. Keeping this heavenly vision before us radically shifts our priority from what we care about to what God cares about. As a result, our soul matures as we become rich toward God and our generosity increases.

This biblical vision for the use of our possessions has largely been lost in the modern world. Rather than being disciples of Christ, we are followers of Mammon. We are saturated in a culture of materialism that takes no thought for God's ownership, our responsibility, and the rewards of eternity. Instead, we are encouraged to accumulate more and more stuff in order to make us happy. How rarely we take time to cultivate gratitude for God's generosity toward us and to practice our own! Believers need a wake-up call regarding the commitment being a disciple of Christ has on your stuff. We hope this book can be that wake-up call.

Ultimately, this book seeks to help you master the critical connection between stuff and the soul in a materialistic culture. We know that the connection between stuff and soul is a critical one because it is mentioned so frequently in God's Word (chapter one) and part of the reason for this is that mastering the connection between stuff and soul is essential to the formation of our souls to enjoy rewards in eternity (chapter two). We master this critical connection by being rich toward God (chapter three), which reorients and redirects our souls toward love of God (chapter four). Once we realize the importance stuff has in regard to our souls, we can discern God's true intentions regarding stuff (chapter five), which helps us avoid the pitfalls that would hinder us from mastering this critical connection (chapter six).

But this is not a joyless task. God promises us rewards for our earthly faithfulness (chapter seven), encouraging us to cultivate patterns of regular giving, both as an individual and as part of Christ's body, the Church (chapters eight and nine). In short, when we master the connection between stuff and soul, we become obedient to the command of our Lord and are able to enter more fully into the joy of our Master (Matt. 25:21).

Our purpose in writing this book is to help you master the connection between temporal stuff and the eternal soul in the middle of a materialistic culture, and we have written *Stuff and Soul* for individual, church, and community group reading. In addition, Personal Applications for Mastery are included throughout each chapter as optional jumping-off points for you to think about and engage with the material, and in the back there are Questions for Mastery to supplement each chapter for small group activities and discussions. These tools are meant to help you use this book as a facilitator of honest conversation between you and God, either by yourself or as part of a small group discussion. May the Spirit lead us into all truth (John 16:13).

Chapter One

---

# STUFF AND SCRIPTURE

*Mastering God's Word on Possessions*

But store up for yourselves treasures in heaven,
where moth and vermin do not destroy,
and where thieves do not break in and steal.
—MATTHEW 6:20

Listen to no man who fails to listen to God.
—A. W. TOZER[1]

Have you ever wondered why there are more passages in the Bible (2,350) about money and possessions than any other topic?[2] Three times more than verses on love, seven times more than verses on prayer, and eight times more than on belief. Almost 8 percent of God's Word in the Bible deals with possessions. Similarly, the largest portions of the parables of Christ (seventeen of the thirty-eight) are about possessions. Why would God focus so much attention on stuff? As a foundation to mastering the critical connection between stuff and soul, it is important to understand the four main reasons why the Bible so frequently mentions possessions: (1) it is a topic very important to God, (2) there is a critical connection between possessions and the soul, (3) God knew it was a topic that would be difficult and challenging for us, and (4) God desires for us to gain eternal rewards in heaven. This chapter will dive deep into these reasons and biblically set the stage for exploring the connection between your stuff and your soul.

## PERSONAL APPLICATION FOR MASTERY

From your perspective, why are there more Scripture references on possessions than on love and faith? Why is it so difficult to be faithful to God's Word in using stuff? How might you change your habits to become more obedient to what the Bible has to say about using stuff?

### 1. It Is Important to God

What is the first, the most important, commandment in Scripture? Jesus tells us that it is to love the Lord your God with all your heart, soul, mind, and strength (Matt. 22:38). This means loving God with everything. Love, real and true love, means giving up yourself in relationship, and this is especially true of our relationship with God and His relationship with us. God gave His only begotten Son to us to justify us completely by His utterly free grace as a gift (John 3:16, Rom. 3:24). And we grow in sanctification, in Christlikeness, by giving of what we have. How can we give ourselves up in love while keeping hold of other things? Can we lay down our life for God while also picking up and holding onto earthly possessions? This insight into God's economy instructs us in the handling of money and possessions and influences our total life's attitude. God wants us to be holy, and to be holy is "to be set apart for God"—and part of being set apart means setting apart. We are to set apart all we are and all we have for God's purposes.

Jesus says that "where your treasure is, there your heart will be also" (Matt. 6:21). Possessions, insofar as we love them, become a part of us, a part we must use to adore Jesus, like Mary did when she "took a pint of pure nard, an expensive perfume ... poured it on Jesus' feet and wiped His feet with her hair" (John 12:3a). Part of being in relationship with God means intentionally using the tools He's given according to His Kingdom purposes. One can only be a faithful steward by the power and presence of the Holy Spirit. God wants us to live in relationship with Him, using our head to form our heart to live, love, serve, and give with open hands.

## 2. A Critical Connection

When Jesus said that our heart is where our treasure is (Matt. 6:21), He showed the vital connection between our stuff and our souls. Where is your heart right now? Ask yourself what and where your treasure is, and you'll know the answer. Sometimes it takes the threat of danger to realize where your treasure really is. When things are tough, what is the most important thing to you? One of Sir Arthur Conan Doyle's Sherlock Holmes stories, "A Scandal in Bohemia," gives us a helpful lesson about locating our treasures.[4] In the story, Sherlock, in order to determine where a woman keeps her important documents, pretends to start a fire in her apartment and then observes where she goes first. He knew that she would immediately go to what was most precious to her—where her precious documents were stored. What do we immediately turn to when things get difficult? What do we take comfort in, and what do we make every effort to save?

Do you want your soul to be stuck here in this life, obsessing over earthly trivialities? Or would you rather that it be focused on heaven "where Christ is, seated at the right hand of God" (Col. 3:1)? As philosopher James K. A. Smith says, "You are what you love."[5] Do you want your soul to be conformed to the image of earthly things or conformed to the image of Christ in heaven? When we allow the Spirit to set our heart and soul on God by using possessions to His glory, we prepare ourselves for heaven, "where moths and vermin do not destroy" (Matt. 6:20) and are being made like Jesus "that He might be the firstborn among many brothers and sisters" (Rom. 8:29). As pastor Chip Ingram says, giving money and possessions "is God's training wheels for growing a generous heart."[6] What we do with our earthly possessions affects our eternal soul. The following chapter will delve more deeply into this critical connection.

## PERSONAL APPLICATION FOR MASTERY

Consider where you are in your spiritual journey and generosity. What practices, people, and surroundings have helped you get where you are today? What has hindered you from progressing further? Make a list of how you might improve on focusing on treasures in heaven.

### 3. A Challenging Topic

God knows how challenging it can be to use stuff in a way that glorifies Him. In the book of Joshua, Achan stole the things devoted to God in the destruction of Jerusalem and incurred God's wrath against the whole camp precisely because of his love of possessions (Josh. 7). It's just so easy to turn a blind eye to how we use possessions and to be pulled into the materialistic economy of the world. *After all*, we like to think, *since we worked long and hard for our things, don't we deserve to use them how we like?* We need God to continuously remind us that stuff doesn't really belong to us, and it matters how we use our Master's things. God in His Word is continuously repeating the importance of using possessions to glorify Him because, when it comes to the call to sacrifice our stuff, we are naturally hard of hearing.

Even though the Bible says so much on stuff, when was the last time you heard a sermon about the spiritual value of being generous with time, talents, or things? God's ultimate ownership of our possessions is seldom taught in churches, and consequently Christian giving is low. Evangelicals give about 4 percent of their income, and all Christians generally give about 2.43 percent.[7] We can see that there is a striking discrepancy between what the Bible says about money and possessions, and how Christians behave with money and possessions.

### 4. Eternal Rewards

God as a loving Father desires for us to gain all the rewards we can get, both on earth and for eternity in heaven. This is a fourth reason why God is so concerned with our stuff. Just like parents on earth desire for their children to get rewards, trophies, and crowns, so God gives us the opportunity to earn rewards for our eternal existence. How we use possessions on earth is of utmost importance because, as 2 Corinthians 5:10 says, "we must all appear before the judgement seat of Christ, so that each of us may receive what is due for the things done while in the body, whether good or bad." Every one of us must appear before Jesus Himself and give an account for how we have used His things.

God entrusts us with stuff as a test of our earthly faithfulness and to determine the rewards we will receive in heaven (1 Cor. 3:10–15; see chapter five (page 41) and the three Ts). God isn't trying to trick you with this test; He wants you to pass with flying colors! Scripture also says that this test not only determines our rewards but also our level of responsibility in God's eternal Kingdom (Lk. 19:11–27). When we use our stuff as the Holy Spirit leads us, in ways that honor Jesus, we are showing God that we can handle heavenly responsibilities. God cares about possessions because he cares about our future lives!

Ultimately the Bible is so focused on money and possessions because of how important they are to your spiritual life. God wants you to use and distribute stuff to His glory in order to more fully enter into His own self-giving life. The Lord "is a God who is jealous about His relationship with you" (Ex. 34:14, NLT), and wants you to be free from earthly anxieties and join in showing His great love to the world. There is a vital connection between honoring God with your soul and honoring Him with your use of stuff. Loving God with stuff is no easy task, which is why God continuously brings the point home to us in His Word. But how does using stuff according to God's Word prepare our souls for a life with Him in eternity? This question will be addressed in the next chapter.

Chapter Two

# IT IS WELL WITH MY SOUL

*Mastering the Idea of Soul*

He refreshes my soul.
—PSALM 23:3

What we do with our resources is a window into our souls.
The question is, what does God see when He looks in?
—R. KENT HUGHES[1]

We all know somebody in Nathan's shoes. Nathan is in his mid-thirties with a wife and three children and a limited income. As you can imagine, things can get pretty hectic around Nathan's house. Many people in Nathan's situation would be tempted to let themselves become obsessed with what they have or don't have and keep a tight fist on their spending. Think of Mr. George Darling from J. M. Barrie's *Peter Pan*. Like Nathan, he's a married father of three with a limited income. Remember how stressed Mr. Darling was with his finances, how he let them consume his every waking moment?

Even though Nathan's familial and financial situation resembles George Darling's, Nathan's attitude is completely different. Listen to his perspective: "My soul is the very core center of who I am, and I view it as a sacred chamber. In this room is a chair deep inside me. In this throne room of life with the empty chair, I can choose what I am going to put on that chair— Christ or bills or stuff."[2] Nathan is different from George Darling because he understands the importance of his soul for loving God.

## PERSONAL APPLICATION FOR MASTERY

How about you? Can you identify with Nathan? What attitudes do you have about your finances? What sits on the chair of your own soul?

But what is a soul, and why is it so important for loving God? There are various perspectives on what a soul is (dichotomist, trichotomist, physicalism, idealism, various dualisms, etc.) and a lot of talk about it by so-called "spiritual" people, but this book will be using the word *soul* as it is defined by *Eerdmans Dictionary of the Bible*: "the life force of living creatures…[and] the seat of the emotions. It is both the center of joy in God (Ps. 86:4) and the seat of the desire of evil in the wicked (Prov. 21:10)."[3] The soul is the part of you that makes you you. It is our life itself, the source of our emotions, volitions, attitudes, and desires, and it is the part of us that continues to exist after death.[4] This chapter will treat three aspects of the soul: the soul as eternal, changeable, and capable of receiving rewards.

### *Your Soul Is Eternal*

In a recent survey, it was revealed that 80 percent of Americans believe in some sort of life after death.[5] But what part of you survives into the next life? The answer is your soul. In Revelation 6:9, for example, the souls of the martyrs are under the altar in heaven waiting for God's justice. Life doesn't end when the heart stops beating. Whether your soul will go to heaven or to hell, you will continue to exist. Of course, even though we are eternal beings, we are not God. Only He is "from everlasting to everlasting" (Ps. 90:2). We are only eternal in one direction; we had a beginning, and we are limited in our capacities. We are forever God's creatures. In addition to this, "all have sinned and fall short of the glory of God" (Rom. 3:23). Our souls aren't just limited naturally, they are utterly dependent on God for salvation. Jesus is the only one who can save our souls and change our eternal destination through belief in Him. Those who believe in Jesus will not have to exist long without a permanent body, however, because there will be a resurrection of the dead where we will receive new, spiritual bodies (1 Cor. 15:20–22). Yet it is because of our souls that humans continue to exist after death.

This has tremendous implications for how we spend our lives in the here and now on earth. We are just passing through—heaven is our eternal home. As C. S. Lewis reminds us, "It is immortals whom we joke with, work with, marry, snub, and exploit—immortal horrors or everlasting splendors."[6] Because we are immortal, what we do here and now in the body impacts our soul for eternity. It makes no sense to acquire wealth now at the expense of eternal joy. As Jesus said, "What good will it be for someone to gain the whole world, yet forfeit their soul? Or what can anyone give in exchange for their soul?" (Matt. 16:26). The well-being and health of the soul is really of incomparable value; our souls are the most valuable things we possess! Nothing else matters in comparison. Of what value is a moment of sinful pleasure compared to eternity? As the martyr and missionary Jim Elliot said, "He is no fool who gives what he cannot keep to gain what he cannot lose."[7]

### *In This Life, We Form Our Souls for Eternity*

Acknowledging the existence of the soul constitutes a whole new way of life. When we realize the eternal nature of the soul, we are freed from worrying about "many things" and can focus on the one thing that is needed—becoming rich toward God (Lk. 10:42). Ruth Haley Barton defines spiritual transformation as "the process by which Christ is formed in us—for the glory of God, for the abundance of our own lives, and for the sake of others."[8] Our souls are vitally important to this spiritual growth in sanctification, since the soul is the place where Christ is formed in us by the Spirit. What we do with our stuff is a way of preparing our souls for eternity and future rewards. When we keep our treasure in heaven and the eternal future of our souls in mind, we form our souls for heaven. As Jesus said, "Where your treasure is, there your heart will be also" (Matt. 6:21). Remember the first and greatest commandment, where Jesus instructs us to "love the Lord your God with all your heart and with all your soul and with all your mind and with all your strength" (Mark 12:30)? This commandment teaches us that the first thing we need to know about the soul is that it is commanded to love God completely.

In God's Word, the soul is the place where desire comes from (Mic. 7:1, Prov. 21:10, Isa. 26:9). Because the soul is both the willing and desiring part of the human person, and because it is eternal, we are shaping our souls right now on the basis of what we love. As philosopher and theologian Paul Wadell says, "We are limited in every way but one—we have unlimited desire, unlimited longing."[9] "[God] has also set eternity in the human heart" (Ecc. 3:11), yet we often look to satisfy our eternal desires and longings in earthly stuff.

But there's good news. The materialistic desires of the heart can actually be transformed by the Spirit into desire for the things of God. Only God in Christ can by His Spirit infinitely satisfy the longings of our souls. We must train our souls to recognize this reality. This concept is constantly referred to in Scripture, where the Psalmist says to his soul, "Praise the LORD, my soul; all my inmost being, praise His holy name!" (Ps. 103:1). We see, by the example of the Psalmist, that it is possible to shape and mold our souls by walking in the Spirit.

Did you ever have the experience of hating something when you were younger but then coming to like it as you got older? Sometimes we simply choose to like something, and by the sheer force of our will, we end up liking it. Our souls function in a similar way. Through the hard work of forming good habits and desires (combined with the life-changing power of the Holy Spirit), we can actually change what we love and long for. Because we can form our souls, we must be cautious of what activities and practices we choose to engage in; not every practice that promises to form your soul forms it in the proper shape! Paul says that the crown of righteousness is awarded to those "who have longed for His appearing" (2 Tim. 4:8). When we are born again, God gives us new desires, and it's our responsibility to grow those holy desires more and more as we seek to minimize our desire for sin. Do you long for Christ's appearing, His coming into this world to set things right? Do you wish you longed for it more? Well, you can!

A fourth-century Christian pastor and philosopher, Gregory of Nyssa, described the soul's desires as a river, and at the end of the river is God.[10] But as the river flows along, part of the water splits off and flows into other channels. Our desires are diverted away from God by things such as food, romance, and material things. All of these are in themselves good, but if we seek them apart from God, they become streams into which the river of our desire flows. Eventually our desire-river is completely dried up before it reaches God. In order for our souls to desire God, we must dry up the other desires so our affections can get to God. We must dethrone everything but God from being ruler of our souls. Only once our desire flows toward God will all these other, lesser loves "be given to you as well" (Matt. 6:33). As we discuss the critical connection between stuff and the soul, it's important to keep in mind that the point isn't your stuff; the point is your soul, and stuff is only the means of soul formation.

The way to keep our desires from being exhausted on our stuff is to steward our possessions for His Kingdom. The point isn't your stuff; it's your heart. As author Chris McDaniel says, "God doesn't want to take 'your' money or TV or car…He wants your heart. He's crazy about you. He wants you to have a love relationship with Him, the God of the Universe. He knows you can't do that if your heart is being pulled and tempted by money and greed."[11] In other words, you have to say "No!" to the things of this world before you can say "Yes!" to the will of God.

### Understanding Your Soul Can Remove Fear

People are naturally fearful. We don't know what tomorrow will bring, and that terrifies us. As pastor and author Gordon MacDonald says, "We must not pretend these fears do not exist, that they are not gnawing at our souls. And we must take a hard look at our tendency to address these fears by simply acquiring a bit more stuff."[12] We can't eliminate our fears by getting more stuff. But knowing that our souls belong to Jesus can help alleviate fear. Since our souls are eternal, we know that this life is not all there is, and that frees us to be unafraid of what tomorrow may bring (Phil. 4:4-7).

Remember Nathan from the beginning of the chapter? Nathan says that "when I put Christ on the chair of my soul, my heart settles and a sense of peace and joy fills my soul. There is an absence of anxieties or fear, and I realize it is really going to be okay. With this resulting joy, I begin to feel connected to what my relationship with

God should be like. FOMO [fear of missing out] goes away."[13] The philosopher Søren Kierkegaard once quipped that "anxiety is the dizziness of freedom."[14] We worry when we realize all the options that lie open before us for what could happen to us and how we could respond. If we choose one activity to do after dinner, that necessarily rules out countless other activities we could have done after dinner. We fear our ability to make choices and the dangers of the world around us. The irony is that we can get so anxious about the choices we make that we never actually make any choices.

This fear is transformed into trust when we, like Nathan, place Christ on the throne of our souls and give Him control of our lives. This is not necessarily something we can do immediately. Learning to trust Jesus with our whole soul can take a lifetime. We are perpetually setting up idols in Christ's place on the throne of our soul. But the battle to rest completely in Christ as conqueror of our anxieties is a battle worth fighting—no matter how long it takes or what we have to give up in the process. When we are free from worry about earthly possessions, we are free for a life of choice, excitement, and adventure.

Often we are tempted to think that we are only called to set apart a certain amount of money, rather than our whole selves. It is not uncommon to hear sermons on giving where the pastor says that God owns 10 percent of your money, and if you give it to Him, He will let you keep the other 90 percent. But this is wrong. God doesn't just own a part of your possessions, He owns all of them. In fact, they're not even your possessions—they're His. This is why it's so foolish to try to accumulate stuff to protect us from the anxiety of not having enough. As Kierkegaard says, possessions "safeguard a person against cares just as well as the wolf assigned to look after the sheep safeguards these against—the wolf."[15] Stuff brings with it its own cares. Even the term "possessions" is a misnomer. We can't really possess anything, since we can't take anything with us when we die. All of these cares weigh us down and keep us from focusing on God. Jesus taught us to pray "give us this day our daily bread" because the bread we eat each day, the water we drink, and the clothes we wear all belong to Him, and we receive them from His hand as a gift day by day. Being aware of the soul frees us from making this life all there is and lets us see all we have as God's good gift to us.

Being free from worldly worry in this way is not only good for us, it is good for all the people we encounter. James, in his Epistle, says that "Religion that God our Father accepts as pure and faultless is this: to look after orphans and widows in their distress and to keep oneself from being polluted by the world" (Js. 1:27). Here is a great mystery: being free from the world and its temptations helps you better love the people in the world. When we keep ourselves unstained by desires and fears, we are actually better able to love and be kind to our neighbors. As the ancient theologian John Cassian says, "With purity of heart the perfection of apostolic love is possessed."[16] If we are no longer enslaved to possessions, we are able to be with people without any secret motive or hidden agenda. We no longer ask, "What's in it for me?" but "How can I serve you?" When we are free from material anxiety, we are free to love one another.

Because our souls are secure in the hand of God through faith in Jesus Christ, we can have courage and confidence to make sacrifices. "Therefore," Paul says, "we are always confident and know that as long as we are at home in the body we are away from the Lord. For we live by faith, not by sight. We are confident, I say, and would prefer to be away from the body and at home with the Lord" (2 Cor. 5:6–8). Peter refers to his death merely as "the removal of my bodily tent" (2 Pet. 1:14, ISV). If our souls are in the hands of God, there is nothing left for us to fear. We can give, save, "spend and be spent" (2 Cor. 12:15, ESV) for the sake of the Kingdom with utter confidence and lack of fear, knowing that this life is not all there is.

Horatio Spafford was so convinced that his soul was in the hand of God that he penned the famous hymn "It Is Well with My Soul."

When peace, like a river, attendeth my way,
When sorrows like sea billows roll;
Whatever my lot, Thou hast taught me to say,
It is well, it is well with my soul.[17]

Spafford wrote these words after the Great Chicago Fire of 1871 destroyed his entire fortune and all four of his daughters drowned with the sinking of the SS *Ville du Havre*.[18] Even though Spafford lost everything, he believed that his soul was eternally secure in the hand of God and was thus able to boldly proclaim, "It is well with my soul." If we believe that our eternal souls are secure in the hand of God, we too can have this confidence.

"The Sinking of the Steamship Ville du Havre" (public domain)

How long do we really have on this earth? A hundred years, give or take a few? This is practically no time at all, compared to eternity. One hundred years is only a long time given a very narrow perspective. God invites us to look at an eternal future and to use these few years to the best of our abilities for the sake of an everlasting Kingdom. As Randy Alcorn says, this life is only a dot on the never-ending line of eternity.[19] We need not be afraid of earthly risk because our souls are eternal, and all that matters is how we use the gifts God gives us. And, based on how we use His gifts, we will receive imperishable rewards.

## PERSONAL APPLICATION FOR MASTERY

Have you experienced sorrows in your life that have tested your faith similar to Horatio Spafford's? If so, in what way have they tested your faith? Can you currently say "It Is Well with My Soul"? Are you living for the dot or for eternity?

### *Our Souls Can Receive Eternal Rewards*

In addition to the crown of righteousness mentioned earlier, which is for those "who have longed for His appearing" (2 Tim 4:8), there are three other specifically mentioned crowns: the crown of life, the crown of joy, and the crown of glory, which are all imperishable (1 Cor. 9:25).[20] These crowns are awarded for different acts of faithfulness. The crown of life is awarded to those who remain faithful under trial (James 1:12, Rev. 2:10), the crown of joy is for those who preach the gospel (1 Thess. 2:19–20, Phil. 4:1), and the crown of glory is for elders and overseers (1 Pet. 5:2–4). In addition to these, there is no reason to think that there won't be additional rewards for other acts of obedience that are not specifically mentioned. For example, in Revelation 1–3, in the letters to the churches, Jesus promises rewards tailored specifically to each church's particular act of faithfulness. We can be confident that if we are faithful with what God gave us, we will be rewarded by Him.

The existence of the soul ensures us that the faithful things we do now will be rewarded by God later on. These rewards are the treasures that we are storing up in heaven "where moths and vermin do not destroy" (Matt. 6:20). At first, it might seem strange to use the promise of rewards as incentives to obedience. After all, if we really loved God, wouldn't we obey Him without a reward? Yes, but that is never a choice we will have to make. God, as the Good Giver, graciously promises us rewards to help us follow Him and as a way of showing us that He is pleased by our obedience. We can thus press on with confidence knowing that if we persevere, we will receive a reward.

In summary, eternal implications follow from what we love and what we do out of that love, so it is important to train our souls to love the right things, "for physical training is of some value, but godliness has value for all things, holding promise for both the present life and the life to come" (1 Tim. 4:8). But what exactly should we do with our stuff to positively impact our souls? The answer is that we must be rich toward God, which we will explore in the next chapter.

# Chapter Three

---

# BE RICH TOWARD GOD

## *Mastering What It Means*

But God said to him, 'You fool! This very night your life will
be demanded from you. Then who will get what you have prepared
for yourself?' This is how it will be with whoever stores up things
for themselves but is not rich toward God.

—LUKE 12:20–21

The object of life, according to Jesus, is breathtakingly simple:
Be rich toward God.

—JOHN ORTBERG[1]

N
o matter if you're a boomer, millennial, Gen X, or Gen Z
person, it is our goal as Christians to be rich toward God.
But what does this even mean? Since God owns it all—the
world, the universe, and all reality—how do we become rich toward
Him? How do you give anything to the one who has everything?
What is the connection?

Let's look at the context of the phrase "rich toward God." In Luke
12:13–21, Jesus tells a parable about a rich fool. In this parable, a rich
man finds that his land has produced bountifully, so he decides to
build bigger barns for his crops and to recline in the lap of luxury.
So far so good. But then God calls him a fool! To God he is a fool,

because he is about to die and the things he worked for all his life are going to perish with him, because he was "not rich toward God" (Luke 12:21).

It is startling that God calls this rich man a fool. Would you consider him foolish? His land produced well, so he maximized resources while he was able to enjoy his well-earned later years in life. To us, this seems like the epitome of earthly wisdom—but God calls it foolishness! All that wealth, all that luxury, is only fleeting. It's here today and gone tomorrow, and you can't take it with you when you die. Just as the preacher says of the rich man in Ecclesiastes, "Everyone comes naked from their mother's womb, and as everyone comes, so they depart. They take nothing from their toil that they can carry in their hands" (Eccles. 5:15).

In the story of the rich fool, we are invited into the wisdom of the eternal Kingdom, which sees wealth in a different light. Through this story, Jesus, like He did for the blind man, spits upon clay and smears it in our eyes (John 9:6). Jesus' parable offends our sensibilities, our wisdom, and our common sense. But it gives us new eyes to see. Riches are transitory and should be used for eternal reasons, for the good of our souls. We find that to be rich toward God is to be "rich in good deeds" (1 Tim. 6:18). In this chapter, we will explore some ways to walk forward with new eyes to be rich toward God.

### *Make Christ the Center*

Being rich toward God means making Christ the center and Lord of every area of your life. It means making Jesus' Way your way. As the renowned theologian Abraham Kuyper said, "In the total expanse of the human life, there is not a single square inch of which Christ, who alone is sovereign, does not declare, 'That is mine.'"[2] Being rich toward Christ is allowing and acknowledging Him as true Lord of each and every piece of ourselves, every crevice of our soul, and every bit of our stuff. And if Christ is the center of our lives, then nothing else can be. "No one can serve two masters" (Matt. 6:24). Early

Christian monks knew this principle so well that in some monasteries it was considered "a great crime" for a monk to refer to any material thing as "my" or "mine".[3] Making Christ the center is not an item on a checklist to be crossed off but a lifelong task and vocation. As author Brian Kluth said, "Declaring God #1 is not just about lip service but about life service—living for Him and honoring Him day by day and week by week with all we are and all we have."[4]

Following Christ's example means humbling yourself like Christ humbled Himself to become dependent on God's provision. As pastor Timothy Keller helpfully notes, "Money ultimately is a form of power, and diminished funds make you feel much less in control of your environment and much more vulnerable to circumstances."[5] We are not just called to give toward God, we are called to be rich toward Him. When we do this, we give up our power like Jesus gave up His power. As Keller notes, "Jesus didn't give because he had power to spare; he gladly lost all his power and became completely vulnerable, for us. What a challenge!"[6] If we are going to be rich toward God, we must make Christ's life our life.

Being rich toward God means keeping our eyes on Christ's example and allowing His Spirit to form our souls and do His will through us. When resources come your way, pray that God will lead you to use them in a Christlike way. When trying to make financial decisions, ask what is most glorifying to God. Strive to have the mind of Christ when you're thinking about buying something new. Try praying for wisdom every time you go into a store. One such prayer you might pray, versions of which have been used by Christians all over the world for centuries, can be found in the Book of Common Prayer:

Almighty God, whose loving hand has given us all that we possess: Grant us grace that we may honor you with our substance, and, remembering the account which we must one day give, may be faithful stewards of your bounty, through Jesus Christ our Lord. Amen.[7]

But be warned! Praying prayers like this one costs something. Following Jesus with how you use stuff might mean not always having the latest and greatest because you chose to feed a family instead. It might mean being teased for not having the best clothes at work because your church needed a new roof. Being rich toward God is about getting your priorities straight. It's knowing that it's more important to give to the poor and stay out of debt than to have the latest and greatest. If you feel outside the camp, remember, that's exactly where Christ is, and we are called to follow Him there, bearing the same reproach which He bore (Heb. 13:13). Being rich toward God, depending on your situation, very well might mean being poor toward the world.

## PERSONAL APPLICATION FOR MASTERY

What does John Ortberg mean when he says, "The object of life, according to Jesus, is breathtakingly simple: Be rich toward God"? Do you agree? Do you find being rich toward God is breathtakingly simple to do? Consider listing actions you might do to become more rich toward God.

### Being Faithful to God's Word

The second area of being rich toward God involves being faithful with what God gives you. In Matthew 25:14–30, Jesus tells the story of a man who went away on a journey and entrusted his property to three servants. Two of the servants invested their master's money and made more, and so were rewarded by their master and commended for their faithfulness. The third, however, chose to bury his talent to keep it safe and was rebuked by the master and cast into outer darkness. The third servant, who chose to bury his master's possessions, was like the rich fool who built bigger barns and reclined in luxury. Both the rich fool and the third servant were concerned with preserving and enjoying their wealth, and both were surprised at their reckoning by their master.

This was because the third servant and the rich man were not faithful to their master's intent. Faithfulness involves the risk and labor of investment. Faithfulness to the Master eschews any concept of playing it safe and hedging your bets. Faithfulness knows no plan B. Being faithful means being more concerned with the Master's will than the Master's money. It's only a tool to do His work. And fidelity, of course, involves an accurate view of the Master "that He exists and that He rewards those who earnestly seek Him" (Heb. 11:6).

Freedom is one surprising element of biblical fidelity. Paul tells us to "let no debt remain outstanding, except the continuing debt to love one another, for whoever loves others has fulfilled the law" (Rom. 13:8). We have to be free from debt in order to be free to give. In order to be faithful to God's Word concerning generosity, we must be free from the external obligations that debt gives, as well as the internal anxieties it produces in our souls. How can we be rich toward God if we have nothing to give because of debt? Debt can keep us from being effective stewards of God's Kingdom and stop us from behaving as God's Word instructs us: "Those who buy something, as though it were not theirs to keep; those who use the things of the world, as if not engrossed in them. For the world in its present form is passing away" (1 Cor. 7:30–31). We must seek to avoid debt because it ties us to a world that is passing away and keeps us from being faithful to the Kingdom that cannot be shaken (Heb. 12:28).

### Being Rich toward God Involves Money and Possessions

It can be tempting to over-spiritualize these concepts. What we must keep in mind is that this theology of stuff is a theology of the particular things we find around us from day to day. We are called to be rich toward God with everything He has entrusted to us and everything we are, and that includes possessions. According to a recent study, millennials often prefer to give time and hospitality as opposed to money or possessions.[8] This is understandable, since millennials often make far below the average boomer.[9] But while hospitality and time are important and still should be given freely, the gift of money and possessions must be added into our lifestyle—whatever your generation. Pope John Paul II said, "Nobody is so poor that he or she has nothing to give, and nobody is so rich that he or she has nothing to receive."[10] Just like the widow who gave her last two copper coins in the temple (Mk. 12:41–44), we are called to put everything entrusted to us at God's disposal, and that involves actively giving to His work in the world.

This principle can be illustrated by Marie. Marie lives well below the poverty line but is committed to give to her local church from off the top, instead of from what's left over. This has put her in some pretty tough situations. Many times, Marie has had to choose between giving to God or paying her bills on time, but she always gives to God first, and God has always supplied exactly what she needs to get by— and then some! Through the generosity of people in her local church, Marie and her husband were given a vacation in Hawaii for their twentieth anniversary, and she is able to send her oldest son to college without going into debt. "It's all about mindset," Marie says. "God is abundantly generous, always more generous than our own generosity."[10] When Marie finds that God has given her even more than usual, she rejoices because she can write a bigger offering check and bless more people. Even though Marie doesn't have much, she rejoices in God's riches toward her and always finds a way to be rich toward Him.

## PERSONAL APPLICATION FOR MASTERY

Do you know people like Marie in your life? What are their characteristics that you admire, and how can you imitate them in becoming rich toward God? What new spiritual practices might you add to your life to become generous as Christ is generous?

## *Be in Intimate Relationship with God*

Being rich toward God involves being in intimate relationship with Him. This relationship between us involves trust. Being rich toward Him involves trusting that God is going to take care of us and trusting that we can be generous because we will be taken care of. But trust in God doesn't just come from out of the blue. It needs to be cultivated through knowing the provider. Spend time in His Word and in prayer. Have fellowship with the saints and confess your sins to one another. Trust God through getting close to Him. As the author of Hebrews tells us, "Keep your lives free from love of money and be content with what you have, because God has said, 'Never will I leave you; never will I forsake you'" (Heb. 13:5). Being free from the love of stuff is about trusting God.

The third servant, who buried his talent, didn't trust his master because he didn't know his master. He only knew part of the story of who his master was—that he was a hard man who reaped what he did not sow. But he had no idea about what his master loved or of the rewards that his master was willing to give to those who took faithful risks. If the servant was in closer relationship with his master, he would have known better what was required of him and what he had to do. His relationship with his master would have empowered him to take faithful risks. As it was, the servant did not know and was not known.

One day, many will come to Jesus and say, "'Lord, Lord, did we not prophesy in your name, drive out demons in your name, and in your name perform many miracles?' And then He will tell them plainly, 'I never knew you. Away from me, you evildoers'" (Matt. 7:22–23). What matters is being known by Jesus, and Jesus knows the ones who do His Father's will (v. 22). Jesus knows those who love the Father, who trust Him completely, and who follow Him. Being free *from* the reign of stuff is about being free *for* relationship with God.

29

## Keep Eternity in Mind

The reason that the rich man was foolish in Jesus' parable is because he didn't keep eternity in mind. He was focused on his present enjoyment and cultivation of temporal wealth. He took no account for his soul, and was not "afraid of the One who can destroy both soul and body in hell" (Matt. 10:28). He thought that this world was all there was. Consequently he shirked his responsibility to distribute what God gave Him to others and be rich toward God.

Todd Harper, president of the Generous Giving ministry, wasn't always so generous. In his book *Abundant,* Todd tells how he underwent a transformation from wanting to make money to wanting to give it away.[11] From childhood on, his early life was dominated by attempts to make money. What really turned things around for Todd was keeping eternity in mind. "It shifted my investment horizon from thirty years to thirty million years."[12] After this transition, Todd assumed the leadership of a generosity ministry called Generous Giving in order to help other Christians transition from greed to giving. Today, Generous Giving hosts the Celebration of Generosity and Journeys of Generosity, which have helped many Christians to become richer toward God. All this came from the simple realization that the things we do here matter for eternity.

"But," we might think, "what about those people who are so focused on heaven that they miss earth? Can you be so fixated on the future that you become slothful or irresponsible in the present? Why care for the poor, or the environment, or about this world at all if it's not our final home and will be destroyed one day?" Remember the stuff and soul connection from chapter one? This world isn't our final home, but the things we do here really matter for eternity. Our rewards, responsibilities, and crowns in the next life will be determined by what we do in this life. The world and people around us are entrusted to our care, and the choices we make concerning them have eternal consequences.

When we say that being rich toward God means keeping eternity in mind, we must remember not to lose touch with our present reality. It's specifically because this life isn't all there is that we should take it even more seriously and be even more concerned with using it well. As the prolific professor and author C. S. Lewis famously said, "If you read history, you will find that the Christians who did most for the present world were just those who thought most of the next ... It is since Christians have largely ceased to think of the other world that they have become so ineffective in this. Aim at Heaven and you will get earth 'thrown in'; aim at earth and you will get neither."[13] Keeping eternity in mind is part of what it means to be rich toward God.

Being rich toward God is not a formula; it's a way of life. The key is to acknowledge the connection between stuff and the soul, and to allow soul formation to translate into stuff sharing. The person who is rich toward God consistently seeks to make Christ the center of their life and allows the concerns of His Kingdom to take preeminence over the concerns of the world. They are intent on being faithful to God's Word and diligently search the Scriptures for what God's will is for their interactions with stuff. They are deeply passionate about their relationship with God and will ruthlessly weed out distractions in that relationship. Finally, they keep eternity in mind, knowing that they will be judged for what is done in the body (2 Cor. 5:10). In the next chapter, we'll examine how being rich toward God spiritually forms us for life with God.

## PERSONAL APPLICATION FOR MASTERY

What are steps you can take to weed-out distractions for you to make Christ the center of your life and to place a greater focus on being rich toward God?

31

Chapter Four

# STEWARDS WITH SOUL
## Mastering *Stuff and Soul* Maturity

Therefore, I urge you, brothers and sisters, in view of God's mercy,
to offer your bodies as a living sacrifice, holy and pleasing to God—
this is your true and proper worship.
—ROMANS 12:1

Spiritual formation for the Christian is a Spirit-driven process of
forming the inner world of the human self–our spiritual side—in
such a way that it becomes like the inner being of Christ Himself.
—DALLAS WILLARD[1]

So far, we have looked into the reality of the soul and the biblical importance of stuff, but what's the connection between the two? This chapter will examine specific ways giving makes your soul more mature through receiving abundant life, moving through faith stages, and inviting you into community.

### Stewarding Is Sanctifying

Now, some readers may be concerned at this part of the book. "Aren't we saved by grace through faith? Isn't this idea of rewards a gospel of works?" No, and for a very important reason. After the Apostle Paul tells the Ephesian church that they are saved completely by God's grace, he says, "For we are His handiwork, created in Christ Jesus to do good deeds, which God prepared in advance for us to do" (Eph. 2:10). Amazing! God has specifically created us for good works that He already planned for us! We are not only saved, we are swept up into the grand adventure of following Christ. We have the opportunity through good works to bless others, become more like Christ, and qualify for eternal rewards.

We could also phrase it like this: justification and sanctification are accomplished in two different ways. Justification is the process through which we are accepted and declared righteous in God's sight by the Holy Spirit's uniting us in faith with the risen Christ—and this happens completely by grace. Our sanctification, on the other hand, is the process by which we become more like Jesus and more like ourselves through the work of the Spirit—and this is a result of God's grace alongside our effort. The rewards we receive are rewards for the good deeds we do in the process of sanctification. While we don't merit our salvation, we can and do merit our rewards, and we will be judged accordingly. As Randy Alcorn says, "While our faith determines our eternal destination, our behavior determines our eternal rewards."[2] This is extremely important for avoiding anxiety over giving and finding joy and encouragement as you do give!

### Abundant Life

Knowing the difference between justification and sanctification can help move us from a scarcity mentality to an abundance mentality. When we are no longer concerned with earning our salvation, and when we are assured of our justification through faith in Jesus Christ, we are empowered to become rich toward God and to enter more fully into Jesus' abundant life of freedom. Jesus came "that they may have life, and have it to the full [or abundantly]" (John 10:10). We can love our neighbors through generosity because God first loved us (1 John 4:19) and was gracious toward us before the ages began in Christ Jesus (2 Tim. 1:9). God's riches toward us inspire us to be rich toward Him; justification fuels generosity! We find in money and possessions an abundance of resources by and through which we can do God's eternal work. Living the abundant life is being abundantly generous with what we have; we graciously give what God has graciously entrusted to us.

A major part of forming your soul is living out your faith—faith that the life of Jesus lived for others really is the abundant life. In justification, God's story is made our story, the story of God's victorious Messiah, Jesus, and His self-giving love. When we are faithful with the possessions God has entrusted to us, we are making a statement about the way things are. We are saying that in the story of humanity, the true God is not riches but the Father of our Lord Jesus Christ. When we walk with the eyes of faith, we see the self-sacrificial life of Christ as the life that is truly abundant, and we reflect this in our own lives by giving. We are taking hold "of the life that is truly life" (1 Tim. 6:19). Because we are justified by faith, we have peace with God through Jesus (Rom. 5:1) and we can trust God the Giver to supply our needs "according to the riches of His glory in Christ Jesus" (Phil. 4:19).

## PERSONAL APPLICATION FOR MASTERY

What are specific areas in your life where you know that God has blessed you? Do you regularly thank God for all these blessings in your life? How might you change your actions to be more reflective to the character of God as Giver of every good and perfect gift (James 1:17)?

Giving is part of the path to holiness, the path of living into the fullness of Jesus' abundant life. This sacrifice demanded of us is not to make us unhappy. Jesus is here to give you life. But Jesus' abundant life is such an enormously massive gift that it needs two hands to carry. We find that we simply can't hold onto our possessions anymore. Jesus knows this is difficult for us. Our giving doesn't go unnoticed; God sees and will reward those who give to His Kingdom (Matt. 6:4). When we are willing to lay down stuff in faith, we are equipped to take up Jesus' abundant life.

## *Stages of Faith and Giving*

| CORRELATION OF STUFF USE AND SOUL TRANSFORMATION | | |
|---|---|---|
| Stages | Faith Characteristics | Evidence in Use of Stuff |
| Stage 1: Imitator | Like a child, is marked by imagination and influenced by stories and examples of others. | Is able to mimic the examples of others in giving when shown or instructed. |
| Stage 2: Modeler | Takes beliefs and moral rules literally. Perception of God is largely formed by friends. | Gives sporadically when given an example to follow. |
| Stage 3: Conformer | Faith becomes a basis for love, acceptance, and identity; involves most aspects of life; and is shaped mainly by relationships. Faith does not yet form a cohesive "philosophy of life." | Gives because it is the thing to do. Likes recognition, tax benefits, and other personal gain from giving. |
| Stage 4: Individual | Begins to "own" one's faith. Faith is less defined by others as one becomes able to personally examine and question one's beliefs. | Starts to give in proportion to what God has given. Danger of becoming prideful regarding giving or giving for the wrong motives. Wonders why others do not give more. |
| Stage 5: Generous Giver | Grasps the main ideas of an individualized faith as well as individual practices. Becomes interested in developing the faith of others. | Recognizes that all one owns is from God. Begins to give of one's own initiative rather than out of obligation or routine. Derives joy from giving. |
| Stage 6: Mature Steward | Little regard for self. Focuses on God and then on others. Free from manmade rules. | Recognizes the role of a faithful steward of God's possessions. More concerned with being rich toward God. Content with daily provision.[5] |

In order to track faith development, it's helpful to have a goal to aim for and markers along the way to know how far you are from reaching your goal. James Fowler's classic model for the stages of faith allows us to do just that. This is not a personality test like Myers-Briggs or the Enneagram; the stages of faith don't try to tell you *who* you are but *where* you are. Your faith stage is not the extent of who you are, but it is a helpful road sign to show you where you are on the way to health and holiness.

Fowler suggests that the individual begins with an intuitive and imitative faith that is mostly built on the examples of others but then progresses to a story- and reciprocity-based faith, where the individual sees himself as part of a story of right and wrong, black and white. Then if he keeps progressing, the individual reaches a synthetic faith, where he is able to integrate his faith with every area of life. From there, he moves to an individualistic model of faith, which is less dependent on others and seeks to know God personally. Then he progresses to a conjunctive level, where he is able to see multiple sides of an issue, until he culminates in the universalizing stage, which happens when individuals are able to fully focus on loving their neighbor and giving up themselves to God's Kingdom.[3]

We can correlate Fowler's stages with stages of being rich toward God, since our faith fuels our giving.[4] We start as an imitator who learns giving from watching others give. We then become modelers who begin to give out of ethical convictions but often go back and forth in our giving and can be judgmental of others. Then comes the conformer stage, where we realize the impact of our giving on those around us but do not realize the deep connection between our stuff and our souls. It seems that most Christians fall into this category. But then if we continue to grow, we pass into the individual stage, where we begin to give more and more and see a right use of possessions as connected to what it means to follow God and form our souls. We stop giving because we have to and start giving because we get to. This pattern increases as we become generous.

We find our giving more and more connected with our spiritual life as we depend more and more on God to supply our needs. Finally we reach the stage of mature steward. Mature stewards give out of conformity to Christ and know that all they have belongs to God and was given to them to bless others. As a result, they are truly rich toward God.

You can see the correlation between Fowler's Stages of Faith and growing rich toward God played out in the chart. Understanding where you are in your faith journey can help you continue to progress "to the whole measure of the fullness of Christ" (Eph. 4:13).

## PERSONAL APPLICATION FOR MASTERY

Do you know anyone in stage 5 or 6 faith stages? What is your current faith stage? What do you think it would take for you to progress to a higher stage? Who might be a like-minded believer with whom you can take this journey together?

### *Forming Your Soul in Community*

Finally, it's important to know that you don't have to worry about forming your soul alone. While Fowler's stages help track individual growth, growth rarely happens individually. Soul formation happens in the context of being with other people, in the family, among our friends, and at church. The formation of our souls, Ruth Haley Barton says, takes place "incrementally over time with others in the context of disciplines and practices that open us to God."[6] When we think about cultivating our souls by giving, we are primarily thinking about how to be the church. It is with the church, the household of faith, that Paul says we should be especially concerned (Gal. 6:10). It is only together that we become a pilgrim people and sojourners in this world. And when we are rich toward God together, we find that generosity occurs in the context of friendship.

As we practice faithful stewardship in community, we have the opportunity to learn from and to teach one another about the generous life. This is never more true than in the context of the family. Husband and wife can mutually encourage one another as they seek to train children to master the connection between our stuff and our soul. A recent Barna study shows that most people who had generous parents will themselves be generous later in life.[7] There are several aids available that can help parents teach their children faithful giving principles, such as The Good Sense Movement's "Raising Financially Freed-Up Kids" (available at https://bit.ly/2J8L0gU).

Teaching children to master stuff for Christ is not the parents' responsibility alone but the task of the entire congregation of believers, by their word and example. As David Kinnaman and Gabe Lyons say, "Jesus revolutionized what it means to be family. In his vision, family isn't limited to biology; it extends to all those who follow him in doing God's will."[8] Christian child-raising happens in a family that is bigger and more diverse than the nuclear family ever could be. And who knows? Maybe we can also learn a thing or two from watching the Spirit's work in our young ones, for "through the praise of children and infants, you have established a stronghold" (Ps. 8:2).

Through stewarding stuff, the Spirit forms the soul by sanctifying and conforming it to the image of Christ. In distributing rather than hoarding our stuff, believers enter into God's abundant life by joining His redemptive mission in the world. This manifests God's power to restore the world to His intended purposes and restores us, bit by bit, in the process. We can chart this transformative gospel growth in ourselves using Fowler's Stages of Faith and labor together in a community to help each other grow in grace as we seek to use God's stuff to God's glory. But how do we glorify God with our stuff? What are God's purposes in giving us stuff? Chapter five will seek to answer these questions.

## PERSONAL APPLICATION FOR MASTERY

What could you do differently to join God's redemptive mission?

Chapter Five

---

# THE PURPOSE
# OF POSSESSIONS

*Mastering the Three Ts*

Then Mary took about a pint of pure nard, an expensive perfume;
she poured it on Jesus' feet and wiped his feet with her hair.
—John 12:3a

The beauty of riches is not in the purse,
but in the power it gives one
to succor those who are in need.
—Philo of Alexandria[1]

Why did God make us stewards if stuff is so difficult to manage? What is its purpose? In this chapter, we'll explore how stuff is good but enticing, and how to redeem stuff by thinking of it in terms of the three Ts: as a tool, a test, and a trademark. This chapter explains what possessions are and what they are to be used for. This does not mean that it's impossible to misuse possessions; you can technically use a screwdriver to clean your ears, though it's certainly not recommended! This chapter seeks to show what possessions are and how to use them according to their true, God-given nature.

41

### *God Made Stuff Good*

An important theme in Scripture is that matter matters! When God created, He called His creation "very good" (Gen. 1:31), and God is going to make, along with the New Heavens, a New Earth (Rev. 21:1). Indeed, the spirit that denies that Jesus Christ really did come in the flesh is the spirit of the Antichrist (1 John 4:2-3). We should not shun the physical things around us as unholy but rather consider them a cause for delight and thanksgiving in God (cf. Ps. 104). Stuff, as part of creation, is good. The problem comes when too much value is placed on possessions or when we use them in a way that doesn't fit with their intended purpose.

Some Christians mistakenly think that stuff is inherently evil, but this is not true. Think about it: if money and possessions are bad, then when Jesus tells the rich young ruler to sell all he has and give it to the poor, the young ruler is giving the poor evil things. That can't be right! Why would Jesus want to give the poor things that would be spiritually harmful to them? No, possessions are God's good creation and can be used for good according to His Kingdom purposes. But this doesn't mean that believers should throw all caution to the wind.

### *Stuff Can Seduce Us*

How can stuff be good but seductive? How could God see the world as "very good" (Gen. 1:31) but then tell us not to love the world or anything in it (1 John 2:15)? The seventeenth-century theologian and poet Thomas Traherne answered this question by saying that there is not one world but two. "One," he says, "was made by God, the other by men. That made by God was great and beautiful. Before the Fall it was Adam's joy and the Temple of [H]is Glory. That made by men is a Babel of Confusions: Invented Riches, Pomps, and Vanities, brought in by Sin."[2] According to Traherne, the world God made good and the world man made bad through sin are completely opposed to each other, and we must "leave the one that you may enjoy the other."[3] Even though God created the world and possessions good, we're still liable to be seduced by them. The world of men, Traherne would say, still has a hold on our hearts. In this life, this "war of the worlds," you can have too much of a good thing or use it in the wrong way. The problem isn't in the stuff; it's in ourselves. Because we are broken on the inside, "prone to wander," we need to be careful about possessions. Remember King Solomon? Because he desired wisdom more than riches, God gave him both (1 Kings 3:10–14). Yet on account of his riches, Solomon broke the law of God and married many foreign women, who turned his heart away from the LORD (1 Kings 11:1–8). Solomon's use of his riches became his downfall, and he ruined the golden age of the united kingdom of his father, David. Perhaps Solomon thought that he could control his wealth or control the religious worship of his wives, but it was really they that controlled him.

The story of Solomon shows us that, when it comes to money and stuff, we are not as strong as we think. Money and possessions, according to Old Testament scholar Walter Brueggemann, are "forces of desire that evoke lust and 'love' in a way that compels devotion and eventually servitude."[4] Stuff powerfully forms our souls for eternity. We can never let our guard down and assume that we are strong enough to use wealth without succumbing to temptation without the Word of God and prayer, by which everything is made holy (1 Tim. 4:5).

### Stuff Can Be Shared

So stuff is good, but it can also lure us away from God. What are we to do? Well, we can diminish stuff's hold on our hearts by giving it away. After all, "Life does not consist in the abundance of possessions" (Luke 12:15). As the biblical scholar Craig Blomberg says, "If wealth is seductive, giving away some of our surplus is a good strategy for resisting the temptation to overvalue it."[5] When we grasp stuff loosely, with open hands, we can actually make far better use of it than hoarding it. This happens when we truly see Jesus. Zacchaeus was a rich man and a tax collector "who wanted to see who Jesus was" (Luke 19:3), and once he met Jesus, he received Him into his house, gave half his goods to the poor, and restored four times what he stole (Luke 19:6, 8). Zacchaeus's riches no longer held his heart because his heart's eyes were enlightened (Eph. 1:18). Once Zacchaeus saw Jesus, he became generous.

One person following in Zacchaeus's footsteps in our day and age is Alan Barnhart. After reading Scripture, Alan became convinced that wealth (1) belongs entirely to God and (2) is entirely seductive. When he and his brother inherited their parents' business, he decided to put certain safeguards in place. They set a "lifestyle finish line," a commitment to give away anything extra over and above their predetermined limits, and they made themselves accountable to a fair salary by their employees. Eventually these measures culminated in them giving 100 percent of their incredibly successful business away to charity. Alan says that they made this decision because the company was "God's company," and they were only stewards. Alan could have been ensnared from his faith by love of wealth, but he chose to be free of that temptation by giving it all away.[6]

## PERSONAL APPLICATION FOR MASTERY

Have you used possessions in a way not pleasing to God? What are specific areas you might change in your life?

On our own, we are not wise enough to use possessions without being used by them. They're too seductive and we're too sinful. To use possessions rightly, we need a greater wisdom than our own—we need Jesus. By looking to Jesus, "who has become for us wisdom from

God—that is, our righteousness, holiness and redemption" (1 Cor. 1:30), we are given the wisdom to use our possessions rightly—by giving them away as Jesus gave Himself away to God's Kingdom. In this way, we can sanctify and redeem stuff through service to God. But what exactly is stuff redeemed for?

In the parable of the shrewd manager, Jesus helps us understand stuff's purpose. In the parable, a master finds that the manager of his resources is not doing his job well. Fearing unemployment, on his last day of work the manager went to all his master's friends and collected on his master's debts—but at a discount to the debtors. If someone owed the master one hundred measures of oil, the manager told him to give the master fifty. The manager carried on like this all day. On the next day, when the manager was out of work, all of his old master's debtors, to whom he gave discounts the day before, became his new friends and were ready and willing to receive and provide for him.

When Jesus is finished telling the parable, He surprisingly praises the manager, saying "The people of this world are more shrewd in dealing with their own kind than are the people of the light. I tell you, use worldly wealth to gain friends for yourselves, so that when it is gone, you will be welcomed into eternal dwellings" (Luke 16:8b–9). How does this parable relate to our stuff? From it, we learn that stuff is meant to function according to the three Ts: as a tool, a test, and a trademark.

### T #1: Stuff Is a Tool

Jesus commends the dishonest manager for his shrewdness and encourages us to make friends for ourselves by our money here on this earth so that "you will be welcomed into eternal dwellings" (Luke 16:9). The people that will receive us into eternal dwellings are all the people that we have blessed with our money. Stuff is a tool by which we can show God's love and preach the gospel. Who will greet you in heaven? Think of all the people who will come up and thank you because of how you blessed them. Our stuff here on earth becomes God's tools for blessing people and doing His work. This is not new for God; He often chooses to use matter to accomplish His purposes throughout the world. His Son, who came in flesh, is remembered by eating bread, drinking wine, and getting wet. So similarly, God uses material possessions in the world as His tools to accomplish His purposes. A. W. Tozer explains:

> A twenty-dollar bill, useless in itself, can be transmuted into milk and eggs and fruit to feed hungry children.... It can be converted into food for the hungry and clothing for the poor; it can keep a missionary actively winning lost men to the light of the gospel and thus transmute itself into heavenly values. Any temporal possession can be turned into everlasting wealth. Whatever is given to Christ is immediately touched with immortality.[7]

God gave us the power and ability to join Him in the quest of His Kingdom and make a lasting impact on the world around us by how we use stuff. The key is knowing how to use it so that it doesn't use us!

How often do we find that, instead of thinking of possessions as tools, we think of them as ends in themselves, as goals? We would think of someone who collected an assortment of hammers as wasting his time if he never actually hit any nails. This would be treating hammers as goals rather than as the tools they are, which are meant to accomplish goals. This is the case not just with those things that are often called tools (like hammers and screwdrivers) but with all stuff. "For we are His handiwork, created in Christ Jesus to do good works, which God prepared in advance for us to do" (Eph. 2:10). Our purpose is not to collect but to do good works, and possessions are our tools.

## PERSONAL APPLICATION FOR MASTERY

Have you ever thought of your possessions as a tool to advance God's Kingdom? What are some resources God has provided you that you could use as a tool? If you have thought of stuff as tools for the Kingdom, who will greet you in heaven as a result of how you used stuff here on earth? How might you change your approach to stuff to be more effective in using it as a tool?

### T #2: Stuff Comes with a Test

Second, possessions are the questions on a test. "What will you do with me?" each one asks. Jesus concludes the parable of the shrewd manager by saying, "Whoever can be trusted with very little can also be trusted with much, and whoever is dishonest with very little will also be dishonest with much" (Luke 16:10). God is watching us to see how we respond to the blessings that He's given us. He's looking for us to be faithful with stuff and to use it all for His Kingdom and His glory. This test determines the rewards, responsibilities, and crowns we will receive in eternity, which will be explored in chapter seven. Like the dishonest manager in the parable, Jesus wants us to think about the future as we use our possessions now—specifically our eternal future. "For we must all appear before the judgement seat of Christ, so that each of us may receive what is due us for the things done while in the body, whether good or bad" (2 Cor. 5:10). God is seeing if He can trust us with much. This test is to discern what it is that we really love because, as James K. A. Smith points out, "You might not love what you think."[8] What we do with possessions is a definitive way to show where our hearts really are.

Since our possessions are a test, it's important that we prepare well by studying hard in God's Word and ask for tutoring. This is not a test that we can afford to blow off or take lightly. But the best thing is that this is an open-book test, and you're allowed to look at your neighbor's answers! We should constantly have our Bibles open when making financial decisions and also ask our friends and neighbors who are further along in generosity for help and guidance. Knowing that we are being tested on our use of money and possessions forces us to take seriously what we do with our stuff and where we are placing our treasures.

## PERSONAL APPLICATION FOR MASTERY

Make a take-home practice test for yourself. After reviewing credit card statements and looking over your possessions, take a sheet of paper and list specific examples that demonstrate that God's eternal Kingdom and your soul's development are your highest priorities. Try to cite five ways that you are leveraging the use of stuff on earth for rewards in heaven.

### T #3: Godly Use of Stuff Is a Trademark

Just as companies often have a phrase or jingle associated with them, God also has a trademark for His followers. His trademark is a generous use of money and possessions. It's easy to see God's character when Christians give to those in need. When Jesus told His parable of the dishonest manager, the Pharisees, "who loved money," ridiculed Jesus for His parable. But Jesus rebuked them, saying, "You are the ones who justify yourselves in the eyes of others, but God knows your hearts. What people value highly is detestable in God's sight" (Luke 16:14–15). The ways of God are not the ways of man. The trademark of sinful man is to justify himself before others, but the trademark of God is to give generously with an eternal future in mind.

In Matthew, Jesus calls Christians "the light of the world" and tells us to "let your light shine before others, that they may see your good deeds and glorify your Father in heaven" (Matt. 5:14, 16). When God's children bear their Father's trademark, their giving becomes a means of others worshipping God. It's not enough for Christians to have the right world view, Francis Schaeffer says, but they must "act upon that world view so as to influence society in all its parts and facets across the whole spectrum of life."[9] We give because God first gave to us, and we are generous as a reflection of His character. When people see us being generous, it shows them the character of God.

A great example of this happened in the early fourth century. The region of Caesarea was experiencing a massive plague and famine, but "all day long some of them [the Christians] tended to the dying and to their burial, countless numbers with no one to care for them. Others gathered together from all parts of the city a multitude of those withered from famine and distributed bread to them all."[10] When the country was in trouble, it was Christians who were compassionate with time and resources. The Christians' "deeds were on everyone's lips, and they glorified the God of the Christians. Such actions convinced them that they alone were pious and truly reverent to God."[11] When the ancient people of Caesarea saw generosity, they recognized God's trademark. This trademark of following Christ was not just something for the saints and martyrs of the past, but it really is for us today! In any situation, we can be known as God's people, and the God of Jesus Christ can be shown to be our God when we use stuff well—to His honor and glory.

## PERSONAL APPLICATION FOR MASTERY

What do people see in your life as examples of generosity? How do you think this bears God's trademark? In what ways could your life better demonstrate God's trademark?

Stuff is and always will be good, but our sinful hearts make mountains out of molehills and turn stuff from a good to The Good, worshipping and serving created things rather than the Creator (Rom. 1:25). The way to free ourselves from our slavery to stuff is to share it with others. When we do this, we turn from being hoarders to God's distributors. This allows us to see stuff in light of the three Ts: to use stuff as a tool to do God's work in the world, knowing that we are being tested as to how well we can bear God's generous trademark to the world. There are eternal consequences to this test, so it is of the utmost importance that we take it seriously and strive to use and enjoy stuff as God intended us to. This is no easy task! Chapter six examines some potential pitfalls that can keep you from mastering the connection between your stuff and your soul.

Chapter Six

---

# STEWARDS BEWARE!

## *Mastering Challenges to Soul Formation*

Jesus answered:
"Watch out that no one deceives you."
—MATTHEW 24:4

I am convinced that the greatest deterrent to giving is this:
the illusion that earth is our home...Heaven, not earth, is my home.
—RANDY ALCORN[1]

When you endeavor to master the connection between stuff and the soul, you find that the way is not all lined with roses. There are thorns here, roadblocks that can keep you from maintaining your goal and can even cause you to lose your convictions if you're not careful. You need to learn how to see these roadblocks and respond accordingly so you aren't hampered or slowed down on your road to giving. In this chapter, we'll look at three challenges to using our stuff: materialism, avoiding the issue, and common practices for raising money. Then comes the hard part: avoiding them in our own lives.[2]

### *Challenge #1: Materialism*

Think about the last time you went to the movie theater. You're sitting there with a cushioned seat beneath you, the warm buttery goodness of popcorn in your mouth. You take a sip of your soda and let your mouth be washed in a wave of sugary sweetness. You scoot to the edge of your seat. The movie is about to start. But what should flash upon the screen but a trailer for another film! You sink back into your seat disappointed, as wave after wave of ads wash over you like your soda washed over your taste buds, saturating you with new desires. You are receptive to these desires—after all, you want to be entertained—and these new wants can only be satisfied by coming back to the movie theater. By the time the movie you paid for starts, you're already planning your next trip. This is the trap of materialism.

Situations like the one just described happen to us day after day without our realizing it. According to the *New York Times*, a person living in a city today is likely to see up to five thousand ads a day, not to mention all the product placement we are exposed to by our friends and neighbors.[3] We see that girl's jeans and think they would look better on us, or we see that guy's new phone and just have to have it. We don't even have to seek advertising out—it ambushes us while we are unawares; constant press surrounds us. It forms and reforms our souls through the stories it tells. Try remembering an instance when a commercial convinced you to purchase a product you didn't know you needed. Pay attention to how the stuff you see in ads affects your emotional and spiritual life. I think you'll be shocked by the prevalent dangers of materialism.

## PERSONAL APPLICATION FOR MASTERY

Name specific advertisements that seem attractive to you but that you know really pull you away from God. How might you avoid being influenced by these advertisements? Have you noticed culture becoming more materialistic? If so, how does culture influence you? What can you do to guard against this influence?

Studies suggest that since World War II, Americans have increased in consumer materialism.[4] Millennials and Gen Z have grown up in their parents' culture of materialism and (particularly in Europe) are more willing to acknowledge themselves as materialistic than older generations.[5]

While materialism has always been a problem for people, it is increasing now in the American context. America started out with the stewardship ideals of the Puritans, who believed that our stuff was entrusted to us by God and we had a sacred responsibility to use our Master's things according to our Master's will. This attitude, however, did not last long.

The country slowly transitioned to a philanthropy mentality, which took God out of the picture and introduced social Darwinism into giving. Stewardship, rather than connoting a transformed heart, lost its meaning and was subsumed into philanthropy. Before, when Puritan stewardship ideals were practiced, giving was indiscriminate to all who were in need. Social Darwinism introduced the idea into giving that only the best and brightest should receive help. Giving, for many in this philanthropic period, was not primarily about honoring God but about advancing humanity.

The downward spiral then continued into our current self-centered period dominated by big government. To modern Americans, stuff seems like salvation and giving like nothing more than a way to get a tax break. Charity is no longer viewed as a practice for individuals and churches but is now an activity of the government. Even the philanthropy mentality of giving to advance the human race has been, for the most part, lost. We don't give to make a difference; we give to feel good about ourselves.[6] According to the work of sociologists Christian Smith and Melinda Lundquist Denton, the majority religion among American youth is "moralistic therapeutic deism," and this phrase characterizes so much of our modern giving.[7] We give because it makes us feel good and we think we probably should, not because we wish to form our souls according to God's Word. Since we have slowly but surely forgotten our theological heritage, we are mired in materialism 24/7.

Sadly the church is not immune to this trend. A recent book by political scientist Mark A. Smith, titled *Secular Faith*, details how culture beat religion in twenty-first century America. His central observation is that "Christians are part of society, not separate from it," and they tacitly accept many modern ideas by either changing their long-standing positions or refraining from expressing their beliefs.[8] Even though Smith does not address the issue of faith and finances, it seems clear that the church has also gone down the culture's secular path. In 2018, only five percent of Christians in America gave at least 10 percent of their income, with the average American Christian giving 2.5 percent of their income (0.5 percent higher than the average American, but 0.8 percent lower than Christian giving during the Great Depression).[9] This issue is so prevalent that the Lilly Endowment's religion division, Economic Concerns Facing Future Ministers, has given millions of dollars to churches, denominations, and pastors to correct the issue.

Materialism is such a big deal because it's a false gospel. Stuff becomes our god and the mall our temple. Commercials and advertisements are the new evangelists for this heresy, loudly proclaiming that "goods and services will save you."[10] Ministry author Mark Vincent notes that money even possesses godlike characteristics, making it easy to idolize. Money is (seemingly) eternal, powerful, and mysterious. It is a force that appears to divinize its devotees and turn broken lives around.[11] Because money seems to share in these godlike qualities, it has become a powerful idol that has gripped both the church and the world. As John Stott says, it can "smother our spiritual life."[12] According to a Barna survey across all generations, only one in ten Christians says that serving God with their money is their number one financial goal.[13] One in ten! It is no surprise that the Israelites in the desert made their famous calf out of gold.

Materialism affects not only how we interact with stuff but also how we view ourselves in connection to other people. Take Helen.

Helen grew up wanting beautiful things. She says she had an unquenchable desire to own every beautiful thing she saw. This led to her becoming angry with her parents for not buying her everything she wanted. Eventually this materialistic desire led her to become obsessed with her body image. She wanted to become "a beautiful thing" just like the beautiful things she hungered to possess, leading her to make false comparisons with others and base her identity on how others could use her. It took Helen years and years of prayer and self-reflection to become free of these early habits and thought patterns.[14]

Helen's story teaches us that materialism is a self problem before it's a stuff problem. Materialism ultimately boils down to what R. Scott Rodin calls "the temptation to be spectacular."[15] Let's face it, being faithful with our stuff is pretty ordinary. It's just simple people responsibly using simple things to do the most unglamorous thing of all: love their neighbors. Materialism tells us that the simple isn't sufficient, that we need to make ourselves more than what God has made us to be. In fact, we can get so caught up in bedazzling ourselves with physical things that we start using other people like we use our stuff. Helen's experience leads her to believe that materialism is the cause of much of the sexual promiscuity that pervades our current culture. Because we use and consume stuff for our own immediate enjoyment, why wouldn't we treat other humans in the same way?

As Christians, we are called to resist our culture and fight against the reign of stuff in our lives. As social critic Neil Postman said, modern advertising "is not a series of testable, logically ordered assertions. It is a drama—a mythology."[16] This means we can't argue because there's nothing to argue against. We can, however, live out a better story, a story where we recognize that how we use our stuff is connected to the life of the soul. This story has consequences; the future and present well-being of our souls is at stake. Again, this is not because possessions are bad. On the contrary, God saw that all of his creation was very good (Gen. 1:31)! It is only when we allow our stuff to take the place of God, as in materialism, that they become an issue. Proverbs 30:8b–9 strikes the perfect balance:

> Give me neither poverty nor riches;
>   but give me only my daily bread.
> Otherwise, I may have too much and disown you
>   and say, 'Who is the LORD?'
> Or I may become poor and steal
>   and so dishonor the name of my God.

Stuff is a gift from God that we should enjoy (1 Tim. 6:17), but we cannot let it take the place of God in our lives.

### Challenge #2: Lack of Good Teaching

The first of Alcoholics Anonymous's famous twelve steps is to acknowledge your present condition. Yet many of us haven't even reached step one in regard to how we think about our stuff and our souls. In order to be rich toward God, we must increase our awareness of what needs to be done and where we're falling short. "Our faith," Princeton sociologist Robert Wuthnow suggests, "has become so narrowly defined that it seldom pricks our conscience when pocketbook issues are at stake."[17] Many people have no idea that God is concerned with how they use their money and that how you use stuff is integral to following Jesus.

Part of the reason for this widespread lack of understanding comes from lack of teaching in the modern Western church on faith and finances. When was the last time you heard a sermon about the relationship between stuff and your soul? It appears that there are two main reasons why there is a lack of teaching on generosity: (1) because pastors are afraid of looking like they're asking for money, and (2) because pastors themselves are confused (seminaries rarely offer courses in this field). In chapter eight, we'll look at ways that the church can turn this situation around, but for now it's important to know that the deficiency exists. Because of the general lack of teaching about money at church, it's important to make a concentrated effort to constantly remind yourself about the soul-stuff connection. You can't just rely on Sunday mornings to be spiritually formed—it's a lifelong affair!

## PERSONAL APPLICATION FOR MASTERY

What misconceptions about the critical connection between stuff and the soul have you had? How have these kept you from being rich toward God? How do you think a right understanding of the critical connection impacts the way you live?

Aside from the lack of church teaching on generosity, another factor that contributes to our confusion is due to the presence of false or misguided teaching concerning stuff. There are some in the church who claim that faithfulness to God always yields earthly riches. They say that you will accumulate earthly riches in direct proportion to your faithfulness to God as a reward here and now. But as the lives of so many Christians have shown, this is not always the case. In Hebrews 11, the great "hall of faith" chapter, we are shown two routes that faith can take. On the one hand, it was those with faith "who conquered kingdoms, administered justice, and gained what was promised; who shut the mouths of lions, quenched the fury of the flames, and escaped the edge of the sword; whose weakness was turned to strength; and who became powerful in battle and routed foreign armies. Women received back their dead, raised to life again" (Heb. 11:33–35a). But then there is another path that faith can take: "Some faced jeers and flogging, and even chains and imprisonment. They were put to death by stoning; they were sawed in two; they were killed by the sword. They went about in sheepskins and goatskins, destitute, persecuted and mistreated—the world was not worthy of them. They wandered in deserts and mountains, living in caves and in holes in the ground" (Heb. 11:36–38). Faithfulness does not necessarily entail earthly abundance.

Think about Jesus. He was faithful to God, and it led Him to death. While counseling a friend once to trust God's providence in his life, he replied, "Look how that worked out for Jesus!" In a way, he was right. Trusting God's plan led Jesus away from earthly riches and glory to His death on a cross. Of course, Jesus is now seated at the right hand of the Father and is King over everything, having "learned obedience from what He suffered" (Heb. 5:8), so things eventually did work out pretty well for Jesus! But He had to suffer and die first. That's the thing about Christianity—it involves death, and lots of it. As New Testament scholar Gary Hoag says, "Christians should abandon 'philanthropy' as that form of giving follows human rules and promises earthly glory."[18] The giving that comes from God doesn't promise earthly glory but the glory that comes from God.

### Challenge #3: Common Practices For Raising Money

The Didache, one of the oldest Christian documents that we have, opens by saying that "there are two ways, one of life and one of death, and there is a great difference between these two ways" (Didache 1:1).[19] The way of God is the way that leads to life, but the outwardly attractive way of the world leads to death. This idea of two ways is especially true in matters of raising money.[20]

We're all too familiar with the world's way of fundraising: aggressive sales strategies, stretched budgets, pressuring clients, and anything that works to compete for a limited amount of money. The world's way is grounded in love of money and the belief that money makes ministry happen. The two ethical guiding questions of the world's way are (1) will it bring in money? And often (2) is it legal? From the world's perspective, donors are philanthropists (rather than stewards) who are to be flattered for their hard work and goaded into giving to gain cultural recognition and thanks. It should be apparent that these practices fail to master the critical connection between stuff and the soul.

When we look at the world's way of asking for money, practiced in so many churches today, we must ask, with Denver Seminary Distinguished Professor of New Testament Craig Blomberg, why is it that ministries that are raising money "do not stress the central biblical truths that giving is a part of the whole-life transformation, that stewardship and sanctification go together as signs of Christian obedience and maturity, and that God will call us to account for what we do with 100 percent of the possessions He has loaned us?"[21]

God's way of fundraising, on the other hand, is very different. In God's way, He is acknowledged as the source and provider of all resources. In His way, we ask and thank Him accordingly, with an understanding that givers are His stewards. These are those whom He graciously invites to participate with Him in His mission in the world. God's way of raising funds focuses on facilitating God's stewards to be rich toward Him, with an ideal outcome that values the spiritual state of the steward more than the monetary value of the gift. God's way is open to the transformation and leading of the Holy Spirit as a motivator for generosity. The whole process, from start to finish, is completed in prayer, with faith that God will provide the needed resources for His will to be done. For more explicit principles about biblical ways to ask for money, see the appendix at the back of this book, "Biblical Principles for Stewardship and Fundraising."

Rich, who has several decades of experience in raising money and working for Christian organizations, has come to adopt God's way of raising resources. He believes ministries should not spend their time asking for money but rather in helping people go to God and see how God wants them to participate in His work. Rich tries to help potential ministry partners identify their passions for God's work and match that passion to ministry opportunities. He tries to help them realize their role as stewards of God's stuff and assist them in being distributors of God's provisions. The goal is for ministry partners to care deeply about giving God's resources. If they don't care, Rich doesn't want them to give.[22]

We can see how opposed the way of God and the way of the world really are! The world's way transacts, God's way transforms; the world's way solicits by manipulation, God's way presents giving opportunities to participate in God's work; and the world's way hoards and stores, God's way enjoys and shares. Christian fundraisers are shepherds of the souls of their ministry partners, not manipulators of a donor; "donor," after all, connotes ownership. Ultimately it comes down to this: God's way acknowledges Him as the true owner of our possessions, whereas the world's way does not. Only when givers are viewed in their fundamental identity as "faithful stewards of God's grace in its various forms" (1 Pet. 4:10) will pleas for money follow God's plan for His stewards' spiritual growth. Ministries should be more concerned with their stewards' inward deepening than with their donations. As stewards on the receiving end of financial appeals, we need the eyes of faith to see God's ways of working in the world and conform to it, rather than to the fundraising practices we see around us.[23]

## PERSONAL APPLICATION FOR MASTERY

Have you noticed that most financial appeals address you as the owner of resources or a donor and not the steward of God's resources? In addition, have you observed that they most often focus on your giving to the organization more than growing your soul to be rich toward God? How might you respond to these appeals from a steward's perspective?

Mastering the connection between your stuff and your soul does not happen automatically. We are surrounded by pressures that seek to form our soul in ways contrary to the way of God. We must be vigilant against these obstacles! Christians must guard against the materialistic culture around them and remember their soul. They must educate themselves concerning the connection between stuff and the soul, and not rely on others to do it for them. Finally, they must evaluate fundraising not according to the world's standards but according to God's miraculous provision for generosity. But do not lose heart, Christian! God woos and beckons us to this risky and dangerous path by the assurance of "His very great and precious promises, so that through them you may participate in the divine nature, having escaped the corruption in the world caused by evil desires" (2 Pet. 1:4). This next chapter will look at God's promises of rewards to those who are rich toward Him.

Chapter Seven

# TREASURES IN HEAVEN

*Mastering God's Reward Program*

For the Son of Man is going to come in His Father's
glory with His angels, and then He will reward each person
according to what they have done.
—MATTHEW 16:27

God will reward you later for your sacrifices now,
for your faith shown now,
for your unselfishness now in this life.
—RON BLUE AND JEREMY WHITE[1]

Nowadays everyone has a rewards program. Everything from
credit cards to sandwich shops to airlines use reward programs to encourage customer loyalty and to incentivize
business. God also has rewards for those loyal to Him. But unlike
the slew of business reward programs, God's rewards are not a mar-
keting scheme to get you to use His product. God wants to provide
rewards to His children for work well done—not because He wants
to trick us into doing His work but because He's a loving Father. In
this chapter, we'll explore heavenly and earthly rewards and what
they'll be like.

### *Earthly Rewards*

Does God ever reward earthly faithfulness here and now? We might very easily be confused about this topic. On the one hand, it is clear from the New Testament that those who claim that earthly riches are always the direct result of earthly faithfulness have departed from the gospel of Jesus of Nazareth, the Suffering Servant. On the other hand, the Old Testament is full of men and women who were faithful to God and as a result were blessed by God with earthly riches. One such person was Solomon, whom we discussed earlier. How are we to make sense of this tension?

First, it's important to realize that there are earthly rewards for faithfulness, but they are different from what we might expect. Jesus says that His true disciples are those who take up their crosses to follow Him (Luke 9:23), and the author of Hebrews characterizes the Christian life as one of discipline (Heb. 12:3–17). When the Old Testament saints received earthly riches, it was not to show us how New Covenant believers would be rewarded here on earth but to foreshadow the spiritual riches of Christ (Rom. 15:4). Many take these promises out of context and use them as a selfish way to earn God's favor and blessing to fulfill materialistic desires. But this is not our story. Indeed, the New Testament even suggests that following Christ and his heavenly reward means spurning earthly riches rather than acquiring them for selfish gain (Heb. 11:26). Instead, the New Testament teaches us to consider "godliness with contentment" as the true gain (1 Tim. 6:6).

## PERSONAL APPLICATION FOR MASTERY

Do you think that you often give to receive an earthly reward, such as public recognition, status, or influence through names on plaques, etc.? What steps could you take to change these motivations? What might you do to begin to see the church as your earthly reward?

But what are the earthly rewards that God gives us? Jesus answers just this question. "'Truly I tell you,' Jesus replied, 'no one who has left home or brothers or sisters or mother or father or children or fields for me and the gospel will fail to receive a hundred times as much in this present age: homes, brothers, sisters, mothers, children and fields—along with persecutions—and in the age to come eternal life'" (Mark 10:29–30). In this passage, Jesus tells us to be rich toward God. As Gary Hoag reminds us, "In ancient thinking, leaving family members or selling houses or fields may represent abandoning that which shaped a wealthy person's identity and what helped them retain the temporal security of their status."[2] To follow Jesus really costs something!

The reward for this earthly fidelity here and now seems to primarily be found in the church and as the church. Our brothers and sisters in the church are the new family we acquire when we renounce our old ones. It is the church's job to provide for one another, so that the person who spends his money for the Kingdom can still have his needs met by another member (Acts 2:44–45, 4:32–35). Notice that we have our new family "along with persecutions." This life is never easy, but we can live it together, and that makes all the difference. God says that "it is not good for man to be alone," and when friends and family forsake us for following Christ faithfully, God gives us a new family, just as God made for Adam "a helper suitable for him" (Gen. 2:18). The earthly rewards of believers are thus supplied through the church as they wait for their eternal inheritance.

### Heavenly Rewards

In addition to earthly rewards, there are heavenly ones. As we discussed earlier, our stuff is a test from God to determine our heavenly rewards. Jesus says, "Whoever can be trusted with very little can also be trusted with much, and whoever is dishonest with very little will also be dishonest with much. So if you have not been trustworthy in handling worldly wealth, who will trust you with true riches? And if you have not been trustworthy with someone else's property, who will give you property of your own?" (Luke 16:10–12). How we steward God's stuff now helps to determine our rewards in eternity.

Heavenly rewards are not some harps or pointless paper crowns. Heavenly rewards are worth having for eternity! They are signs of honor that are imperishable and eternal that we will receive after the final judgement for our acts of service here in this life. As mentioned in chapter two, these rewards will include crowns and other items specific to particular acts of faithfulness. These are the treasures you've been storing up in heaven "as a firm foundation for the coming age" (1 Tim. 6:19) through a godly use of stuff. Thus there will be different levels of rewards that Christians will receive in heaven (Matt. 25:19–23), and there is also reason to believe that rewards already in your heavenly bank account can be lost (Matt. 25:29). This serves as a tremendous motivation for hard work and faithfulness. Followers in Christ need not be slaves to our desire for things in this world because they have the opportunity to earn better, eternal possessions in heaven (Matt. 6:20).

Just imagine. God is the Giver who gives us sunrises and sunsets every dawn and dusk, and who gave His only Son Jesus to save us. God knows how to give good gifts and how to reward those who seek Him (Heb. 11:6). If you want to know that God can pick out good gifts, just look around you: "Every good and perfect gift is from above, coming down from the Father of the heavenly lights, who does not change like shifting shadows" (James 1:17). All the riches lavished upon the Old Testament saints were to hint at the extreme gifts that God has in store. They were temporary; these are eternal. Because of the promise of heavenly rewards, we can truly have confidence that "it is more blessed to give than to receive" (Acts 20:35).

Whenever we give, we should consider our heavenly rewards. In fact, the ancient pastor Basil of Caesarea says that when you give to the poor, what you're really doing is giving out a loan, because God will repay with interest everything you give to those in need.[3] Randy

Alcorn calls this "The Treasure Principle": "You can't take it with you—but you can send it on ahead."[4] This is why the audience of the book of Hebrews was able to joyfully accept the plundering of their property; they had "better and lasting possessions" (Heb. 10:34).

Basil and Alcorn's idea of getting back what you give to God is supported by Proverbs 19:17, which reveals that "whoever is kind to the poor lends to the LORD, and He will reward them for what they have done." Giving is an investment opportunity that pays fruitful dividends; it should really bring us excitement to give! Because of God's overabundant repayment of our generosity, Basil advises us to "distribute your wealth lavishly" in order to "keep everything with you when you go!"[5] The only way to take your wealth with you when you die is to use it in the service of God and His gospel.

## PERSONAL APPLICATION FOR MASTERY

Is your giving motivated by earthly rewards from culture or are you motivated to give by God's promise of eternal rewards? Do you await the repayment of investments you've made in this life in the next? What decisions could you make now that would yield fruitful dividends in eternity?

It's important to remember, however, that God's rewards do not work on a transactional basis. "The kingdom of heaven does not operate on the basis of commercial convention. God rules by grace."[6] Just because we earn God's rewards doesn't mean they aren't still His free gifts. Even the opportunity to be rich toward God comes from God (1 Chron. 29:14)! Jesus illustrates this point in Matthew 20:1–16 with the parable of the laborers. A manager of a vineyard hires laborers at the beginning of the day and also hires additional laborers near the end of the day. When the day is over, he pays both sets of laborers the same amount. As the manager, he has the right to be gracious to those employees who came late. This is how God's rewarding works. God's rewards are better than fair. They're grace.

Because rewards are God's gifts, however, it means that we can lose them. Pastor Keith Krell lists six ways that you can lose your rewards:

> First, we can forfeit rewards by seeking them from men (Matt 6:5–6; John 5:44). Second, we can have rewards taken from us because of our unfaithfulness (Matt 25:28). Third, we can become disqualified for rewards because of moral and spiritual compromise (1 Cor 9:24–10:11). Fourth, we can lose rewards because of an unproductive life (1 Cor 3:15). Fifth, we can lose rewards by carelessness and waste (2 John 8). Lastly, we can have our rewards taken from us because of lack of attention to the obedient life (Rev 3:11).[7]

The loss of heavenly rewards should serve as an excellent motivation for us to be faithful over what God has given us.

But what about our giving? If you're thinking about rewards when you give, doesn't it cease to be a true gift? Doesn't the gift lose value if you're planning on receiving something in return? No, because it is God our Father who promises to reward us. God the Father is concerned with our holiness and discipline, and He promises rewards to help us along. Perhaps C. S. Lewis said it best:

> If there lurks in most modern minds the notion that to desire our own good and earnestly to hope for the enjoyment of it is a bad thing, I submit that this notion has crept in from Kant and the Stoics and is no part of the Christian faith. Indeed, if we consider the unblushing promises of reward and the staggering nature of the rewards promised in the Gospels, it would seem that our Lord finds our desires not too strong, but too weak.[8]

God wants us to truly hope for and desire rewards in heaven. It only becomes wrong and greedy if we seek the gift apart from the Giver.

This wrong and greedy seeking of the gift rather than the Giver is exactly what happened in the parable of the prodigal son in Luke 15:11–32. The prodigal son wanted to use his inheritance apart from his father, and his older brother wanted a party with his friends without thought for his father. But the father explains to his son, "You are always with me, and everything I have is yours" (Luke 15:31). Both sons wanted what was already theirs in relationship with their father, but they wanted the gifts apart from the giver. This was where they went wrong.

The father's gifts are good and should be desired, as long as the sons seek them in relationship to him. The gifts which the father gives to his prodigal son are soon dispersed once he leaves home. They vanish by the son's reckless living and a famine in the land (vv. 13–14). As soon as the prodigal returns, however, the father's gifts are waiting for him—a robe is put on his shoulders and a ring on his finger and the fatted calf is killed for a feast (vv. 22–23). In the parable, it's the father's delight to give his sons good things, and it's the same with our Father![9] Heavenly rewards are good to desire specifically because they are heavenly, that is, continuously in the presence of God. When we desire heavenly rewards, we are desiring the Father's presence.

Because God is a loving Father, He desires to give good gifts to His children! He shows His Fatherly favor and approval of our actions by promising rewards for earthly faithfulness in using stuff. This should serve to spur us on to love and good works, sharing and giving away our possessions in the joy that comes from knowing what lies ahead. Yet God's abundant goodness is not constricted to the afterlife but breaks forth into the present through the gift of His Church to individual believers, supplying fathers to the fatherless, children to the barren, and lands to the destitute. These earthly rewards herald our future heavenly bliss and the rewards that will follow. By sharing our possessions, we are securing for ourselves new and better ones in the presence of God. But the rewards of God are only given to those who do the work of God. The next two chapters will examine how to practically master the soul and stuff connection, both in community and individually.

Chapter Eight

---

# ONE BODY, MANY MEMBERS

*Mastering the Art of Giving Together*

I hope to come to you soon, but I am writing these things
to you so that, if I delay, you may know how one ought to
behave in the household of God, which is the church
of the living God, a pillar and buttress of the truth.
—1 Timothy 3:14–15

[The church] exists…to set up in the world a new sign
which is radically dissimilar to [the world's] manner and
which contradicts it in a way which is full of promise.
—Karl Barth[1]

While everyone is called to master the critical connection between stuff and the soul, no one is called to do it alone! The art of being rich toward God should be modeled by pastors and church leaders to their congregations. This chapter can be beneficial both for laypeople and pastors.

Pastors, you can take inspiration from these suggestions to make the church into a more generous community. Laypeople, you can suggest these strategies to your church leadership and offer up your service in their implementation. Consider whether you would be willing to head up a lay committee or host a Bible study in your home.

These are real ways that laypeople can put the material in this chapter into practice at their local church. Here are ten ways to turn the tide in the culture's lack of care in matters of your soul and stuff. While this isn't a foolproof equation, the steps have repeatedly proved helpful and can start you thinking on specific steps your congregation can take to increase in mastering the connection between stuff and the soul.

## PERSONAL APPLICATION FOR MASTERY

In what ways would you be willing to get involved to facilitate generosity and stewardship programs at your church? Which of the suggestions in this chapter seems the most appropriate to accomplish at your church? What steps could you personally take to see that it gets done?

### 1. A Written Philosophy of Money and Possessions

It's important for your church or Christian organization to have a clear financial direction to make sure everyone is on board and united in an effort to master their money. A shared biblically sound statement of purpose and a roadmap for the future aid in the creation of generous communities. It's imperative to have both a shared vision and a shared theology, a place where you're headed and a plan on how to get there. You can have the best intentions in the world, but it's also important to have a plan for implementation to make sure things actually get done!

Steward professionals, such as Rich from chapter six, who have decades of experience in helping churches attest to the importance and power of a written biblical philosophy of ministry developed from Luke 12:21 ("be rich toward God").[2] With such a statement, pastors can encourage their congregations, and congregants can encourage and hold their church leadership accountable. It is important that this plan be theologically grounded. The church's practice of raising stewards must never be divorced from the theological conviction that our use of stuff forms our souls. Charity without soul formation is cheap. Theology need not divide a church; it can actually bring people together in pursuit of a common goal. You can find some biblical principles outlined for the creation of just such a document in the appendix "Biblical Principles for Stewardship and Fundraising" or in the statement on money and possessions found in *Revolution in Generosity*.[3]

### 2. Pastoral Training in Giving

Since many seminaries don't offer courses in responsible use of possessions, it's important for pastors and church leaders to take the initiative in understanding the soul and stuff connection. It's essential not only to give but to know how to give effectively and wisely. Like the noble Bereans, search God's Word for what it says about the soul and stuff connection (Acts 17:11). Apprentice yourself to an experienced giver in your congregation and listen to them and look up to them in their giving. Refer to the correlation of faith stage levels in chapter four. Once you are trained, you'll find yourself better equipped to train others. Laypeople, if you read an interesting book on giving and generosity, recommend it to your pastor! None of us are so far along that we can't use a little help.

Pastor Chip Ingram took this very path in his own development as a steward. He recounts how, as a young pastor, he came in contact with an elderly man who was a tremendous giver in his congregation. The man gave Chip $5,000 to distribute to those in need. Through distributing this money and being in relationship with this man, Chip was formed into a mature giver. It was through this relationship that Chip learned the connection between his stuff and his soul.[4]

Although our exact situations may differ from Chip's, we can all draw on the wisdom of people in our local church communities.

### 3. Don't Treat Money from a Resource Raising Perspective

As we discussed in chapter six, many modern ways of raising money are unbiblical and lead to confusion in the congregation. As noted in *Outcomes* magazine, "to align with Kingdom-focused excellence, a ministry's actions around raising resources will seek a desired outcome to grow givers or stewards who have hearts rich toward God (Luke 12:21)."[5] Money is a sacred trust and should not be treated manipulatively or frivolously. Congregants should not be viewed as donors but as ministry partners. Seek transformation of hearts and soul growth first, and that will then result in giving.

Thus lay people should not be flattered, tricked, or goaded into giving by their pastors but addressed frankly from the perspective of the good of their souls. When the church is asking for money, she must remember that there is no spiritual value in spectacle; making a manipulative and public show out of giving is ultimately harmful to everyone. Giving is not about the money or budget, it's about the spiritual growth of the giver.

### 4. Regularly Preach the Biblical Theme of the Soul and Stuff Connection

"For God so loved the world that he gave ..." (John 3:16). From cover to cover, the Bible is filled with the theme of generosity, and it's not hard to spot or preach once you're looking for it. In the Garden, God gave Adam every tree of the Garden to eat except one, and that is the one Adam ate from. From the third chapter of Genesis, we are confronted with God's generosity and our ingratitude. Further, when God graciously gave Israel the Promised Land, He commanded them that, just as they received generously from him, so they must show generosity toward others (Deut. 10:19). All throughout God's cosmic story of redemption, His restoration of His gift from our ingratitude, runs the theme of generosity and the call for us to be rich toward God as He is rich toward us. If we wish to declare the whole counsel of God (Acts 20:27), we must declare that "it is more blessed to give than to receive" (Acts 20:35).

If the stuff and soul connection is not preached from the pulpit, it probably won't be lived out in the congregation. The truth must be proclaimed both in word and deed. If a pastor is a generous person but doesn't preach about the relationship between stuff and the soul, the congregation has no context for their pastor's actions. The pastor's giving can't be a living illustration of this principle if the principle isn't already known! This is why it's so important for pastors to not only live out the generous life but to preach it from the pulpit.

### 5. Create Lay Committees That Oversee Financial Programs

When Moses was in the wilderness, he was overwhelmed with work, and at the advice of his father-in-law Jethro and the permission of the LORD, he appointed elders to aid him in the task of ruling the people (Exod. 18:13–27, Num. 11:16, Deut. 1:9–18). In a similar way, it can be overly burdensome and exhausting for church staff to oversee programs, and it can be helpful to form a committee of laypersons. These laypersons can then oversee development and brainstorm ways of encouraging your specific congregation to give, while growing themselves in responsibility and understanding themselves. If you're a layperson, don't just wait for this to happen, take the initiative!

## PERSONAL APPLICATION FOR MASTERY

In what ways has God uniquely gifted you so that you can bless His Church? How might you contribute your gifts into making your church a more generous community?

### 6. Form an Inter-social and Integrated Education System for Stewards

It's important to create a culture of generosity. Day after day, we're exposed to a culture of greed and hoarding. It's important for the church to be a place where we realign our heart, mind, soul, and strength into the truth of mastering the soul and stuff connection. Chris Willard and Jim Sheppard claim that "the culture of the church is the most powerful way of effecting corporate change."[6] A culture of generosity can be encouraged through forming inter-social and integrated education groups. Let millennials and boomers, men and women, and rich and poor learn and teach each other together. The church can cultivate a culture of being rich toward God by committing to mastering the soul and stuff connection in community together.

Take Soren, for example. Soren is a millennial who often gives in large amounts sporadically, whenever he hears of someone in need of help. Soren understands the deep connection between stuff and his soul and wants to lessen materialism's hold on his life. But Soren is not a regular or consistent giver. "My generosity mostly just looks like a general looseness with money, but I want to be a more habituated giver and feel my loss more consistently."[7] Soren and other millennials could really learn from older generations who are more disciplined givers, and perhaps older generations could learn from Soren's youthful energy and willingness to be instantly generous to God's Kingdom work at the drop of a hat. The church should capitalize on and make the most out of these differences.

### 7. Use Outside Resources

Your church doesn't have to walk the path of stewardship alone! Roger Lam, who wrote a book detailing his testimony, said that it was during a Crown Financial Ministries presentation at his church that "the pin dropped" for him in connection to his responsibility as a steward.[8] "It's not that I had not heard what was said before," Lam says, "but it finally *really* sank in that *everything* I have belonged to God."[9] Sometimes an external stimulus can help get the message across. These parachurch ministries can provide the backbone to a group project or discussion that pastors can supplement with their own wisdom and experience. These resources can also help reinforce that the connection between stuff and the soul is not something unique to your church but is a value that is shared by Christ followers everywhere!

### 8. Make Use of Tools That Encourage a Variety of Ways to Give

With the advent of the internet, there are now an assortment of ways to give that your church can take advantage of. For example, a Barna study found that 39 percent of practicing Christian millennials give over the internet at least once a month, and two out of ten donate over text at least once a month.[10] It's worth looking into implementing modern technology, such as church apps and online and text donations, to give people every opportunity to give. Your ministry can make use of these tools to give the most people the opportunity to give to your church. If you are particularly tech-savvy, consider donating some time to your church to help them set up these new electronic ways to give.

### 9. Regularly Communicate the Church's Financial Position to Congregants

A culture of generosity is built on honesty and openness. Pastors should let people know how the church is doing financially. Ministry is not about the budget but about growing generous hearts to be rich toward God. People should have the opportunity to rejoice together when the church is doing well and also to meet the needs that are around them. Pastors shouldn't be shy about being transparent with their church's finances! The church is the people of God doing the work of God, and asking for money gives congregants the opportunity to earn eternal rewards. We are all baptized into one body, says Paul, and that body has not one, but many members (1 Cor. 12:13–14). Our sorrows and our joys should be common, and also the responsibility to help when we can. The church blesses her members by helping them bless each other. Remember, pastor, you are not asking for yourself, but as the Lord's embassy for the Lord's work.

### 10. Pray for a Revival in Mastering the Soul and Stuff Connection

The most important thing we can do, of course, is pray. John Wesley once famously quipped that "God does nothing but in answer to prayer."[11] While the exact theology of this quote is debatable, the sentiment is certainly valid. "Ask and it will be given to you; seek and you will find; knock and the door will be opened to you" (Matt. 7:7). There's a power in prayer, and Christians need to take more advantage of it. Pragmatics without prayer is a problem waiting to happen. Because of the intercession of the Son (Heb. 7:25) and the Spirit (Rom. 8:26), we have an all-access pass into the throne room of grace, which we can approach boldly with all confidence (Heb. 4:16). The church needs a wake-up call about our use of money, and it's our job to pray that God wakes us up!

The local church is the schoolhouse of our faith. It's where we learn the ABCs of prayer and fasting and the 1-2-3s of evangelism and discipleship. The church can make the most of her teaching role by equipping the saints with the necessary tools to do God's Kingdom work. Teachers should begin with a teaching method and educational philosophy, and the church is no different. Then the teachers must be trained. Likewise pastors should take charge of their education so that they might better teach their congregants.

## PERSONAL APPLICATION FOR MASTERY

Has anyone ever mentored you about what God says about stuff? If so, what did they teach you? If not, who in your life could mentor you? How might you serve as a mentor to others, or encourage like-minded believers?

The church, if she is going to teach well, should be consistent in her message and practice, refusing to treat money from a worldly money raising perspective and regularly preach God's Word about being rich toward Him. The church should seek to get everyone involved in this educational program, creating lay committees and inter-social and integrated education systems. The church should not be afraid of using outside resources and tools but make the most of every opportunity to help form people's souls into the image of Christ. Finally, the church should engage in open communication about her financial situation with her members and also with God in prayer. When the church is faithful, she empowers her members to go and do likewise in their own personal lives, which we will explore in this next and final chapter.

## Chapter Nine

# WALKING THE WALK

*Mastering Our Stuff in Real Time*

God loves a cheerful giver.
—2 CORINTHIANS 9:7

A man's life is always more forcible than his speech.
When men take stock of him they reckon his
deeds as dollars and his words as pennies.
If his life and doctrine disagree, the mass of onlookers
accept his practice and reject his preaching.
—C. H. SPURGEON[1]

astering the connection between our stuff and our soul is a two-part process: cultivating a generous heart and then actually being generous. "For Jesus," says R. Scott Rodin, "generosity is an attitude of the heart long before it is a description of an act."[2] Here are some tips on how to adjust your attitude to be rich toward God out of an abundant and cheerful heart.

### 1. Declare That Jesus Is Lord

As we discussed previously, generosity is a trademark of the Kingdom of God, and it's time we acknowledge Jesus as our King. We need to be committed to the Lordship of Christ above every other master. To say that Jesus is Lord is to say that everything else is not. If Jesus is Lord, then we must consider all else as loss and absolute rubbish (Phil. 3:8). We are saved by this verbal confession, along with heart belief in Jesus' Lordship over the greatest of all His rivals—death (Rom. 10:9), and we are sanctified by allowing this truth to transform our lives.

Jay experienced this transformation in his own life. He relates how the understanding that Jesus is Lord of everything completely changed the way he lived his life. "I came to understand that I needed to take better care of God's body that I was living in. I realized that I wasn't raising my children—I was raising God's children. It hit me that my time wasn't mine to do what I wanted; it was God's time for me to do what He wanted. I saw that I had been entrusted with His gospel to steward it to carry out His Great Commission. I also needed to be careful how I cared for the earth that belongs to Him. And my talents were not mine, they were His. The more I studied, the more all-encompassing the concept of stewardship became."[3] Like Jay, we too can be transformed by the realization that Jesus is Lord over all.

## 2. Acknowledge the Problem of Culture

It's hard to fight a spiritual battle if you don't know what you're up against! Our culture does not acknowledge the absolute Lordship of Jesus Christ over our money and possessions. Instead it asserts that money and possessions have lordship over Him. If we are going to resist the pull of the culture, it's imperative that we know how materialistic it really is and how it's seeking to pull us away from Jesus' costly way of discipleship. The culture presents to us the easy way of idolatry. We must be diligent in fighting this battle for our souls and following God's command to "worship the Lord your God and serve Him only" (Luke 4:8).

## 3. Know the Soul and Stuff Connection

If we forget about the connection between stuff and our soul, we'll become susceptible to the pull of our culture. We need to continuously be reminded of the spiritual connection that possessions have. Moses instructed the people to bind the commandments of God on their hands, heads, doorposts, and gates. They were supposed to be continuously talking about them and teaching them to their children (Deut. 6:7–9). We are in continuous need of being reminded of the connection between our possessions and our soul. This is one reason it's so important to regularly spend time in prayer and with God's Word. We need a constant reminder that worshipping God is not only spiritual, it involves our stuff.

Tim and Julie practice the soul and stuff connection by listening attentively to the voice of the Holy Spirit.[4] It was during a Bible study that they felt convicted about their giving, and now they yearn for His guidance and strive to follow His leading with their use of stuff. This includes increasing their giving 1 percent each year. When they listen for the guidance of the Holy Spirit, they are acknowledging the incredibly close connection between their giving and the formation of their souls through obedience. As a result, they have found themselves growing closer to their community and more willing to take faithful risks. Richness toward God means leaning into Jesus' abundant life.

### 4. Understand What a Generous Heart Looks Like

Humans are imitative creatures. We find out who we are and how we should behave primarily from other people. This is not just true of children but of all people of all ages. This is why Paul tells the Corinthian church, which doesn't have many spiritual fathers (1 Cor. 4:15), to "follow my example, as I follow the example of Christ" (1 Cor. 11:1). Generosity is primarily caught, not taught! It's important to have examples of what generosity looks like. You can find role models for generosity both in salvation history (Heb. 11) and in your local church community (Heb. 10:25). Having past and present role models in being rich toward God can help you avoid making mistakes and find encouragement. It can be easy to feel that you're alone in your commitment to generosity, and having examples can help remind you that you are "surrounded by such a great cloud of witnesses" (Heb. 12:1).

This was Alice's experience. When Alice was a sophomore in college, she was in crisis because she couldn't afford to continue school. She came to church one Sunday in tears, and her pastor asked her what was the matter. Once she explained the situation, he immediately agreed to help her pay for school out of his own personal finances. This shocked Alice and made a lasting impact on her. Alice grew up in a home where giving was viewed transactionally: if I do something for you, you have to do something for me. The pastor demonstrated selfless giving with no strings attached. He demonstrated the stuff and soul connection. Since then, Alice tries to follow her pastor's example and uses everything she has to form her soul in accordance with God's Word. It was through her pastor's faithfulness with his finances that Alice learned how to be rich toward God. We all have the potential to be learners and teachers in mastering the soul and stuff connection.[5]

### 5. Count Your Blessings

Gratitude is not just for the day before Black Friday. "Count your blessings, name them one by one," the old hymn tells us.[6] Make a list of things you have to be grateful for. This is old advice, but it still works! You just might be surprised by your abundance of blessings. When we see how much God has blessed us and is blessing us, it inspires us to bless others as we are blessed. If you try to give while feeling cheated or robbed, then your gift will not proceed from a cheerful heart but from clenched fists, a stiff neck, and gnashing teeth. The theologian Karl Barth said that "radically and basically all sin is simply ingratitude."[7] Practicing thankfulness can help us keep from sin and inspire in us a heart of generosity. It takes a grateful heart to be a giving heart.

### 6. Give Cheerfully

In 2 Corinthians 9:7, Paul tells us that "God loves a cheerful giver." We should not give out of compulsion but out of our abundance. We should want to give! The ability to give is a good gift God Himself gave to His Church. If you find yourself not cheerfully giving, it can help to reorient your perspective on giving. The Church Father Maximus of Turin said, "Joyful, therefore, and cheerful is the one who attends to the poor. Quite clearly he is joyful, because for a few small coins he acquires heavenly treasures for himself."[8] Change your perspective on giving from a "have to" into a "get to" and you will slowly start to find yourself more cheerful as you give.

### 7. Give Secretly

"So when you give to the needy, do not announce it with trumpets, as the hypocrites do in the synagogues and on the streets, to be honored by others. Truly I tell you, they have received their reward in full" (Matt. 6:2). Rather than letting people know about our giving, we should do it in secret so that we're not doing it for our own ego or reputation. When you give, be so discreet that your right hand doesn't know what your left hand is doing (Matt. 6:3). When we give discreetly, it helps us give from a joyful heart, rather than an attention-seeking and proud heart.

Of course, it's not enough to just cultivate attitudes of giving—you need to actually give! Here are some quick tips on practical outlets where you can master the soul and stuff connection.

### 1. Give to God First—Just Do It!

After reading a book like this one, it can be easy to fully intend to give to God but never actually end up doing it. Don't let this happen to you! Make a plan and put it into action; give to God systematically. Start planning on how best to use His resources. The heart transformed by God can't help but boil over into giving. Many Christians through the centuries have found that the Old Testament tithe of 10 percent is a good starting place for giving (realizing, of course, that not only the 10 percent but the 100 percent completely belongs to God). Creating a plan for giving can help make sure you start this discipline. This does not mean you have to be tied down with your giving. You should also be open to meeting spontaneous needs. Millennials tend to be more likely to give spontaneously than older generations, who tend to give according to a plan.[9] Both these approaches are important, and people in different generations can learn from each other. Both planned and spontaneous giving can be led by the Spirit, and a combination of both can be a healthy way to grow in Christ. Remember, giving is not a transaction but a heart transformation.

## PERSONAL APPLICATION FOR MASTERY

Do you believe you are to be generous as Christ is generous? Reflecting upon your life, are you pleased with the quantity and quality of your generosity? Do you believe you are being obedient and faithful to God's expectations for your life as a steward?

## 2. Give According to Your Means

Being rich toward God will look different for everyone. You shouldn't judge how much you should give based off someone else's gift. Everyone's resources vary. Giving any specified amount might be a tremendous sacrifice, or it could barely make a dent in your income. King David would not offer to God sacrifices that did not cost him anything, and we should make the same commitment (2 Sam. 24:24). To truly follow Jesus, we should give generously, but cheerfully and without compulsion. Finding this balance will look different for everyone, but it should always be according to your means.

Lee and Diane are a couple blessed by giving according to their means. They believe there are no coincidences in God's economy and it is important to pay attention to the small things that God provides. Lee and Diane feel the more they give, the more they are blessed. They believe there is a deep spiritual reality underlying how they use the resources God entrusts to them, and because of their faithfulness, they can cite story after story of how God's eternal Kingdom is advanced as a result of their giving from what God gave them.[10]

## 3. Give Regularly

Giving can't just be a mountaintop experience but should be a spiritual discipline that characterizes your whole life. As Kyle David Bennet says, "There can be no disciples without discipline. There can be no true image bearers without instruction."[11] If we want our souls to be shaped by giving, we should make a habit of it. Jesus commands us not to take up our cross once in a while when we feel like it, but "daily" (Luke 9:23). It takes discipline and perseverance to continue using God's resources in a God-honoring way. To start this habit, it might be helpful to set up regular withdrawals from your bank account as a direct transfer to your church and other ministries. Giving costs us, and we will naturally stop doing it if we are not committed and habituated into that discipline.

## 4. Give Regardless of Your Circumstances

If we let our circumstances determine how we give, we'll never actually end up giving anything. We'll always find that our money and possessions never quite meet our standard of living, so we will delay giving a little longer. Instead we need to commit to give to God first, not from what's left over. Think about giving from the gross rather than the net. Consider the example of the Macedonian church in the first century. Paul says that "in the midst of a very severe trial, their overflowing joy and their extreme poverty welled up in rich generosity. For I testify that they gave as much as they were able, and even beyond their ability" (2 Cor. 8:2-3a). Now that's generosity! The Macedonian church knew their possessions weren't their own but belonged to God. Because of this, even in their poverty they rejoiced in "the privilege of sharing in this service to the Lord's people" (2 Cor. 8:4). Let us follow their example and strive to "excel in this grace of giving" (2 Cor. 8:7c).

## 5. Give as a Family

Giving isn't an individual activity, it's a team sport! Seek to give as a community and as part of a family. Mastering the stuff and soul connection as a family binds your hearts together in a common goal and direction. Consider pooling your resources to make a gift. Try praying together as a family and letting your children have input in what causes and institutions your family supports. This teaches children to value and respect giving from an early age and can bring the whole family together in a common commitment to mastering the connection between stuff and the soul.

Mastering the soul and stuff connection means growing holiness in attitudes and actions. We allow the absolute Lordship of Jesus to transform every aspect of our thoughts and emotions. All the same, we must be diligent in acknowledging the downward pull we feel all around us, tempting us to settle for making lesser loves, lesser things, Lord of our life. We fight this pull by reminding ourselves of the incredibly close relationship between our soul and our stuff, keeping before us models of what generous hearts look like. If the bad examples of materialistic culture can do so much damage to our soul, imagine how much good can be done from dwelling on the good examples of the church! We are reminded to count our blessings and remember the lavish and extravagant love God has already shown us. This empowers us to give cheerfully and quietly in full knowledge that our gifts are seen and will be rewarded.

These attitudes then find expression in giving. The Spirit is not bound to spontaneity but is just as free to operate within a God-honoring plan. We should train ourselves, bit by bit, to honor God according to our means and regularly give regardless of our circumstances as a way of forming our souls to consistently love God with all we are. When we live this way, both individually and in community, we worship God and proclaim His Kingdom among the nations.

## PERSONAL APPLICATION FOR MASTERY

What are three specific changes you will make in your life to be more generous, as Christ is generous?

# CONCLUSION

O ur prayer for you is that you have become inspired to master the critical connection between stuff and your soul. We have made the case that how you use stuff forms your soul for eternity. Money and possessions are mentioned so often in God's Word because they are a means by which we can express faith, hope, and love in God with all of our heart, soul, mind, and strength (chapter one). The soul, as this book used the term, is the location of our affections and the part of you that is formed for eternity by our earthly activities (chapter two). The way we love God with our souls is called being rich toward God, which proclaims allegiance to King Jesus and fidelity to His Word by faithfully using stuff in a way that allows us to be in intimate relationship with Him (chapter three). When we are rich toward God, it actually changes the character and loves of our very souls (chapter four), and teaches us to view stuff according to God's intended purposes for it as a tool, test, and His trademark in the world (chapter five).

Choosing to love God with everything we have, however, is no easy task. We encounter the obstacles of materialism, ignorance, and unbiblical fundraising, which can turn our focus away from Christ and His Word if we let them (chapter six). God encourages us to press on through these difficulties by promising us rewards, both on earth (to a limited extent in the church) but most especially and boundlessly in heaven (chapter seven). Finally we begin this important task of mastering the soul and stuff connection by cultivating our attitudes to giving by being transformed by His gospel and allowing our attitudes to bubble over into practical generosity both in community and every day of our lives (chapters eight and nine).

Take a look around you. Take note of the things you see. None of them will be with you in eternity. You will be with Jesus in eternity. Cling to Him, make Him your treasure. Allow Him to transform your perspective and the way you interact with stuff on a day-to-day basis. As the hymn says,

"And the things of earth will grow strangely dim, in the light of His glory and grace."[1]

# A GROUP STUDY GUIDE

This guide seeks to create the opportunity for individuals to hold each other accountable within the context of a supportive group with the goal of being rich toward God. As these groups process the biblical material and content of this book, members should strive to become deeper Christian disciples with a more biblical perspective on stuff and soul issues. The steps below aim to facilitate fruitful conversation about the day-to-day practice of mastering the critical connection between stuff and the soul. Group participants are encouraged to read the corresponding chapter and begin practicing its instructions before the meeting, and to share their experiences, questions, and challenges with one another as they seek to live out their obedience to God's Word. Ideally, in each successive meeting, individuals will report how they are improving in their mastery as Christian disciples of the critical connection between stuff and soul.

## *Chapter One:* STUFF AND SCRIPTURE

**Read:** Stuff and Scripture: Mastering God's Word on Possessions

**Pray:** To better understand why stuff matters to God and to your soul.

**Reflect:** On the following Scripture passages: Matt. 6:19–21, Matt. 22:38, Luke 19:11–27, John 12:1–3, 1 Cor. 3:10–15, 2 Cor. 5:10, Col. 3:1–4.

**Discuss:**

1. Why is stuff so important to God?

2. Share how you have sought to "love the Lord your God with all your heart and with all your soul and with all your mind." (Matt. 22:37) when you use stuff. Can you offer one or two suggestions on how you could improve this area of your life?

3. Do you find it uncomfortable to talk about the connection between stuff and the soul? If so, why might that be?

4. What emotions do you associate with appearing before the judgment seat of Christ (2 Cor. 5:10)? Does this future give you hope? Does it scare you? Why?

5. Is there one instance in your life, or the life of someone you know, that God might reward in the next life?

**Act:** At this point in your life, what are one or two steps you could take to master the place of stuff in your life?

## *Chapter Two:* IT IS WELL WITH MY SOUL

**Read:** It Is Well with My Soul: Mastering the Idea of Soul

**Pray:** That God would help you love Him with all your soul.

**Reflect:** On the following Scripture passages: Ps. 23, Ps. 103:1–2, Isa. 26:9, Matt. 16:24–27, 2 Cor. 5:1–10, 2 Tim. 4:7–8, James 1:27.

**Discuss:**

1. Can you commit to try in the days ahead to treat each person you encounter as an everlasting being? Come to the next meeting ready to share about your experience.


2. What things in your life would you be willing to remove to get closer to God? Challenge yourself to think of something you could give up tomorrow, just for the day, in order to create space for God.

3. Would you describe yourself as an anxious or fearful person? How has stuff (or lack thereof) played a part in causing anxiety or fear?

4. How have you grown in love for Christ and longing for His return throughout your Christian life?

5. Why do you think God rewards our obedience?

**Act:** List three specific ways to give greater attention to your soul health by how you use stuff.

## *Chapter Three:* BE RICH TOWARD GOD

**Read:** Be Rich Toward God: Mastering What It Means

**Pray:** That God would show you how to be rich toward Him.

**Reflect:** On the following Scriptures: Ecc. 5:15–16, Matt. 6:24, Matt. 25:14–30, Mark 12:41–44, Luke 12:13–21, 1 Cor. 7:30–31, Heb. 13:5, Heb. 13:11–14.

**Discuss:**

1. Why did Jesus condemn the rich man in Luke 12:13–21?

2. In what ways are you like the rich fool? How might making Christ the center of life help make you rich toward God?

3. Does being rich toward God necessarily involve giving stuff away?

4. How would you currently define the status of your relationship with God? How has this relationship been noticeably helped or hindered by how you have used stuff?

5. How does knowing you will die one day change the way you live and use resources?

**Act:** Name two things you are going to do differently to focus on being rich toward God.

## *Chapter Four:* STEWARDS WITH SOUL

**Read:** Stewards with Soul: Mastering *Stuff and Soul* Maturity

**Pray:** That God will reveal your spiritual state to you and lead you toward growth in Him.

**Reflect:** On the following Scriptures: John 10:7–10, Rom. 12:1, Gal. 6:10, Eph. 2:8–10, Eph. 4:11–13, 1 Tim. 6:17–19, 1 John 4:7–21.

**Discuss:**

1. What are the differences between justification and sanctification? How are they connected?

2. How has Jesus' abundant life flowed into and transformed your life?

3. Examine the chart of Fowler's faith stages (page 36) and provide examples of people you know in each stage. Are you willing to share your current stage of faith with the group? What specific steps have you taken to advance from one faith stage to another in your spiritual journey? What steps could you take to move to a higher faith stage?

4. How has your church community, positively or negatively, impacted your spiritual development? Do you have to go to church to be rich toward God?

5. If you have children, what is your approach to teaching the connection between stuff and the soul to your children? What are some of the obstacles to showing your children how to use resources in a godly way?

**Act:** What faith stage are you at now, and where would you like to be? Make a list of five specific steps you can take in the next year to help you progress to a higher faith stage.

## *Chapter Five:* THE PURPOSE OF POSSESSIONS

**Read:** The Purpose of Possessions

**Pray:** That the Holy Spirit would teach you how to use stuff according to His purpose.

**Reflect:** On the following Scriptures: Gen. 1, Matt. 5:14–16, Luke 16:1–15, Luke 19:1–10, 1 Tim. 4:4–5, 1 John 2:15–17, 1 John 4:2–3.

**Discuss:**

1. How can God call everything He made good (Gen. 1:31) but also tells us not to love the world or anything in it (1 John 2:15)?

2. How have you found possessions to be seductive toward sin this past week?

3. Are Christians morally obligated to share their stuff? How could you share with those in need?

4. Make a brief inventory of the major tools God has given you to accomplish His work in the world. Brainstorm how different resources could be used as tools.

5. Who is someone you know who bears God's trademark of generosity? How might you imitate them?

**Act:** What are one or two areas of your life you can change so that generosity can become your trademark?

## *Chapter Six:* STEWARDS BEWARE!

**Read:** Stewards Beware!: Mastering Challenges to Soul Formation

**Pray:** That God would give you wisdom and discretion to use your stuff to avoid pitfalls.

**Reflect:** On the following Scriptures: Prov. 30:8b–9, Heb. 11:32–38, Deut. 30:15–20, 1 Pet. 4:10–11, 2 Pet. 1:3–11.

**Discuss:**

1. What is the most dangerous roadblock in your life to using God's stuff in God's way?

2. How have material things kept you from being as rich toward God as you could since the last meeting?

3. What are some ways that materialism impacts your faith? How can you fight back against a culture of materialism?

4. When was the last time you heard a sermon about stuff and your soul? Did you put what it said into practice?

5. Have you ever received a financial appeal that made you feel guilty? Do you think this is a biblical tactic? Why or why not?

**Act:** Share one or two specific things that you will do differently this next week to address these roadblocks in your life. Also, consider what things your church could do differently to help you grow your soul in generosity.

## *Chapter Seven:* TREASURES IN HEAVEN

**Read:** Treasures in Heaven: Mastering God's Reward Program

**Pray:** That God would increase your longing for heavenly treasures.

**Reflect:** On the following Scriptures: Prov. 19:17, Matt. 16:27–28, Matt. 25:14–30, Mark 10:29–30, Luke 15:11–32, Heb. 11:24–26, 1 Tim. 6:6–10.

**Discuss:**

1. Do you think God has ever given you an earthly reward for faithfulness? Why or why not?

2. How has Christianity meant death for you?

3. How can you trust that God's heavenly rewards are worth the sacrifice?

4. Can you truly give a gift to someone else while expecting a reward from God?

5. Describe the story of the prodigal son in your own words. How might the story of the prodigal son have gone differently if the sons had realized that the gifts of their father came in relationship with him?

**Act:** Make a plan to do something before the next meeting that you think God might reward in heaven.

## *Chapter Eight:* ONE BODY, MANY MEMBERS

**Read:** One Body, Many Members: Mastering the Art of Giving Together

**Pray:** That God would join your church together in love, giving you wisdom and insight in how you can be rich toward Him together.

**Reflect:** On the following Scriptures: Ex. 18:13–27, Deut. 6:4–9, Acts 17:10–11, 1 Cor. 12:12–26, 1 Tim. 3:14–15.

**Discuss:**

1. How has your local church modeled being rich toward God?

2. If your church has a written philosophy of money and possessions available, print it and bring it to the group. How would you summarize your church's philosophy of money and possessions? (Possibly consider inviting a pastor or church officer to come and share the church's philosophy of giving).

3. Would you still give money if you were appealed to with an unbiblical fundraising strategy? Why or why not?

4. What have you learned from someone in a different generation about giving?

5. How might your small group make a difference in helping your congregation master the critical connection between stuff and the soul?

**Act:** In light of the content of this book, discuss one or two specific ways that your church might change and become more biblical about how it teaches its members to be faithful stewards

## *Chapter Nine:* WALKING THE WALK

**Read:** Walking the Walk: Mastering Our Stuff in Real Time

**Pray:** That God would give you the strength to do His will.

**Reflect:** On the following Scriptures: Matt. 6:2–3, 1 Cor. 11:1, 2 Cor. 8:1–3, 2 Cor. 9:6–15, Phil. 3:7–8.

**Discuss:**

1. What are some blessings that you are thankful for, and how might these examples encourage you to be generous?

2. How can you give so that your right hand does not know what your left hand is doing (Matt. 6:3), while at the same time letting your light shine before others (Matt. 5:16)?

3. Do you tend to give impulsively or systematically? How could you integrate both approaches into your giving?

4. What are reminders you can set for yourself to give regularly?

5. When it comes to giving, how can parents and children help each other?

**Act:** List three main lessons you have learned by studying how to master the critical connections between your stuff and your soul and give specific examples of what you are going to change in order to form your soul for eternity.

# APPENDIX

## *Biblical Principles for Stewardship and Fundraising*

In 2003, a national task force of twenty-three Christian leaders was convened under the joint auspices of the Christian Steward-ship Association (CSA) and the Evangelical Council for Financial Accountability (ECFA). Chaired by Wes Willmer, the purpose of the task force was to develop these biblically based principles, which were approved by both boards.

Christian leaders, including development staff, who believe in the gospel of Jesus Christ and choose prayerfully to pursue eternal Kingdom values will seek to identify the sacred Kingdom resources of God's economy within these parameters:

1. God, the Creator and sustainer of all things and the One "who works within us to accomplish far more than we can ask or imag-ine," is a God of infinite abundance and grace.
2. Acknowledging the primacy of the gospel as our chief treasure, Christians are called to be stewards and managers of all that God entrusted to them.[3]
3. A Christian's attitude toward possessions on earth is important to God, and there is a vital connection between how believers utilize earthly possessions (as investments in God's Kingdom) and the eternal rewards that believers receive.[4]

4. God entrusts possessions to Christians and holds them accountable for their use as a tool to grow God's eternal Kingdom, as a test of the believer's faithfulness to God, and as a trademark that their lives reflect Christ's values.[5]

5. From God's abounding grace, Christians' giving reflects their gratitude for what God has provided and involves growing in an intimate faith relationship with Christ as Lord of their lives.[6]

6. Because giving is a worshipful, obedient act of returning to God from what has been provided, Christian fundraisers should hold a conviction that, in partnership with the church, they have an important role in the spiritual maturation of believers.[7]

7. The primary role of a Christian fundraiser is to advance and facilitate a believer's faith in and worship of God through a Christ-centered understanding of stewarding that is solidly grounded in Scripture.[8]

8. Recognizing it is the work of the Holy Spirit that prompts Christians to give (often through fundraising techniques), fundraisers and/or organizations must never manipulate or violate their sacred trust with ministry partners.[9]

9. An eternal, God-centered worldview promotes cooperation rather than competition among organizations and places the giver's relationship to God above the ministry's agenda.[10]

10. In our materialistic, self-centered culture, Christian leaders should acknowledge that there is a great deal of unclear thinking about possessions, even among believers, and that an eternal Kingdom perspective will often seem like foolish nonsense to those who rely on earthly kingdom worldview techniques.[11]

When these principles are implemented, which rely on God changing hearts more than on human methods, the resulting joy-filled generosity of believers will fully fund God's work here on earth.[12]

1. Matt. 6:19–21; Matt. 6:33
2. Gen. 1; Ps. 24:1; Col. 1:17; Eph. 3:20; Ps. 50:10-12; Phil. 4:19; 2 Cor. 9:8; John 1:14; Heb. 1:3
3. Rom. 1:16; 1 Cor. 9:23; Phil 3:8–11; Matt. 13:44; Matt. 25:14–46; 1 Pt. 4:10; 1 Cor. 1:18; 1 Cor. 1:23-24; Matt. 28:18–20; Gen. 1:26–30
4. Matt. 6:24; Matt. 22:37; 1 Tim. 6: 6–10; Phil. 4:17; Matt. 19:16–30; Luke 14:12–14; 1 Cor. 3; 2 Cor. 5:10; Eph. 2:10; 1 Tim. 6:17–19; Matt. 25:31–46
5. Luke 16:1–9; Lev. 19:9–10; Deut. 14:22–29; Deut. 24:19–22; Is. 58:6–7; Gal. 2:10; 1 Cor. 16:1; 1 Cor. 9:14; 2 Cor. 8:14–15; 2 Cor. 9:12; Js. 2:15–16; Heb. 13:15–16; 1 Tim. 6:17–19; Mal. 3:10; Matt. 6:24–33; Luke 12:15–34; Matt. 25:14–46; Eph. 2:10; John 15:8–10; John 15:12–17; John 13:34–35; Matt. 22:34–40; 2 Cor. 8:9; Gal. 6:10; Col. 3:17; 1 Tim. 6:18
6. Mark 12:41–44; Luke 12:16–34; Gen. 14:20; Ezra 2:69; Luke 7:36–50; 2 Cor. 9:10–12
7. 1 Chron. 29:10–14; Rom. 12:1; James 3:1
8. 2 Tim. 3:16–17; Exod. 34:32; Exod. 35:21
9. John 15:4–5; Isa. 32:15–17; Isa. 34:16; John 15:16–17; John 15:26; John 16:13–14; John 6:63; John 14:15–21; 1 Thess. 1:2-6; 1 Thess. 2:13; Gal. 5:16–25; Rom. 12:4–8; 1 Pet. 1:2; Neh. 1:4–2:8; Isa. 55:8–11; 2 Cor. 9:5–7; 1 Chron. 28:6; 1 Chron. 29:9; Prov. 21:1; 2 Cor. 3:5
10. 2 Cor. 4:16–18; 1 Cor. 3:1–9; Phil. 4:7; Gal. 5:13–25; Ps. 90:1–12
11. 1 Cor. 1:17–31; 1 Cor. 2:1–5; 1 Cor. 2:14
12. Exod. 36:6-7; Matt. 6:10; 2 Cor. 9:8–12

For more information, see Joyce Brooks, "Appendix: Understanding and Applying Biblical Principles for Stewardship and Fundraising" in *Revolution in Generosity: Transforming Stewards to be Rich Towards God,* ed. Wesley K. Willmer (Chicago: Moody Publishers, 2008), 401–423.

# NOTES

## Introduction

1. Cf. James Wallman, *Stuffocation: Why We've Had Enough of Stuff and Need Experience More Than Ever* (New York: Spiegel & Grau, 2013).
2. R. Scott Rodin, *Stewards in the Kingdom: A Theology of Life in All Its Fullness* (Downers Grove, IL: InterVarsity Press, 2000), 20.

## Chapter One

1. A. W. Tozer, *The Root of the Righteous* (Chicago, IL: Moody Publishers, 2015), 21.
2. Mark Lloydbottom in *Foundation Truth on Money and Possessions: Consider the Source. Read, Listen and Reflect on the Biblical Truth* (Your Money Counts: UK, 2016), 2.
3. Daniel Conway, *What Do I Own and What Owns Me?: A Spirituality of Stewardship* (New London: Twenty-Third Publications, 2005) 18, as quoted by Betsy Schwarzentraub in *Giving: Growing Joyful Stewardship in Your Congregation*, volume 20 (Richmond: EMS, 2018), 35.
4. Sir Arthur Conan Doyle, "A Scandal in Bohemia" in *The Adventures of Sherlock Holmes* (Digireads.com Publishing, 2015), 5–22.
5. James K.A. Smith, *You Are What You Love: The Spiritual Power of Habit* (Grand Rapids, MI: Brazos Press, 2016).
6. Chip Ingram, *The Genius of Generosity: Lessons from a Secret Pact Between Two Friends* (Madison, MS: Generosity Church, 2011), 83.
7. Ruth Moon, "Are American Evangelicals Stingy?" in *Christianity Today*, Jan 31, 2011. https://www.christianitytoday.com/ct/2011/february/areevangelicals stingy.html

## Chapter Two

1. R. Kent Hughes in *Philippians: The Fellowship of the Gospel* (Wheaton: Crossway, 2007), 190.

2. From a personal interview, used by permission.

3. Henry L. Carrigan, Jr. "Soul" in *Eerdmans Dictionary of the Bible* ed. David Noel Freedman, Allen C. Myers and Astrid B. Beck (Grand Rapids: Wm. B. Eerdmans Publishing Co., 2000), 1245.

4. J. P. Moreland, *The Soul: How We Know It's Real and Why It Matters* (Chicago, IL: Moody Publishers, 2014), 45–46.

5. Maggie Fox, "Fewer Americans Believe in God—Yet They Still Believe in the Afterlife," 2016. https://www.nbcnews.com/better/wellness/fewer-americans -believe-god-yet-they-still-believe-afterlife-n542966.

6. C. S. Lewis, *The Weight of Glory* (San Francisco, CA: HarperOne, 2001), 45–46.

7. Recounted by Elisabeth Elliot, *Through the Gates of Splendor* (Lincoln, NE: Back to the Bible Broadcasts, 1981), 172.

8. Ruth Haley Barton, *Life Together in Christ: Experiencing Transformation in Community* (Downers Grove, IL: InterVarsity Press, 2004), 29.

9. Paul J. Wadell, CP, *The Primacy of Love: An Introduction to the Ethics of Thomas Aquinas* (New York: Paulist Press, 1992), 61.

10. St. Gregory of Nyssa, *On Virginity*, chapter 7. Accessed at http://www.newadvent .org/fathers/2907.htm.

11. Chris McDaniel, *Ignite Your Generosity: A 21-Day Experience in Stewardship*, (Downers Grove, IL: InterVarsity Press, 2015), 20.

12. Gordon MacDonald, *Generosity: Moving Toward a Life That Is Truly Life* (Madison, MS: Generous Church, 2009), 30.

13. From a personal interview. Used by permission.

14. Søren Kierkegaard, *The Concept of Anxiety: A Simple Psychologically Orienting Deliberation on the Dogmatic Issue of Hereditary Sin,* trans. Reidar Thomte and Albert B. Anderson (New Jersey: Princeton University Press, 1980), 61.

15. Søren Kierkegaard, "The Cares of the Pagans": *Christian Discourses; and a Crisis in the Life of an Actress: Kierkegaard's Writings XVII,* trans. Howard V. Hong and Edna H. Hong (Princeton University Press, 1997), 23.

16. John Cassian, *The Institutes*, trans. Boniface Ramsey, OP, Ancient Christian Writers (New York: The Newman Press, 2000), 102.

17. Horatio G. Spafford, "It Is Well with My Soul" in *Hymns for the Family of God* (Nashville: Paragon Associates, Inc., 1976), 495.

18. C. Michael Hawn, "History of Hymns: 'It Is Well with My Soul'" https://www. umcdiscipleship.org/resources/history-of-hymns-it-is-well-with-my-soul.

19. Randy Alcorn, *Money, Possessions, and Eternity* (Carol Stream, IL: Tyndale House Publishers, 2003), 102–103.

20. See Joe L. Wall, *Going for the Gold: Reward or Loss at the Judgement of Believers* (Houston, TX: Xulon Press, 2005), 137.

## Chapter Three

1. John Ortberg, *When the Game Is Over, It All Goes Back in the Box* (Grand Rapids: Zondervan, 2009), 27.
2. Abraham Kuyper, *Sovereiniteit in Eigen Kring* (Amsterdam: J.H. Kruyt, 1880), 35.
3. John Cassian, *The Institutes*, 84.
4. Brian Kluth, *7 Keys to Open-Handed Living in a Tight-Fisted World: How to Transform Your Life and Change the World for the Glory of God* (Self-published), 25.
5. Timothy Keller, "Financial Scarcity + Gospel Joy = Riches" at timothykeller.com (12/18/08). http://www.timothykeller.com/blog/2008/12/27/financial-scarcity -gospel-joy-riches.
6. Keller, "Financial Scarcity + Gospel Joy = Riches" http://www.timothykeller .com/blog/2008/12/27/financial-scarcity-gospel-joy-riches.
7. 1979 *Book of Common Prayer* (New York: Church Publishing, 1979), prayer #38, 827. Modified to modern English.
8. Barna Research Group, *The Generosity Gap: How Christians' Perceptions and Practices of Giving Are Changing - and What It Means for the Church* (Barna Group, 2017).
9. Cf. Ben Steverman, "America's Millennials are Waking Up to a Grim Financial Future," https://www.bloomberg.com/news/articles/2018-06-21/america -s-millennials-are-waking-up-to-a-grim-financial-future
10. Pope John Paul II, in *Bread for the Journey: A Daybook of Wisdom and Faith* by Henri Nouwen, reading for April 2 (San Francisco: HarperCollins, 1997).
11. From a personal interview, used by permission.
12. Todd Harper, *Abundant: Experiencing the Incredible Journey of Generosity* (Self-published, 2016), 9–32.
13. Todd Harper, *Abundant*, 21.
14. C. S. Lewis, *Mere Christianity* in *The Complete C.S. Lewis Signature Classics* (New York: HarperOne, 2002), 112.

## Chapter Four

1. Dallas Willard, "Living a Transformed Life Adequate to Our Calling," 2005 address to the Augustine Group. Cited in Gary Hoag, "We will do what we are," 6/29/2016. https://generositymonk.com/2016/06/29/dallas-willard-we-will-do -what-we-are/

2. Randy Alcorn, *The Law of Rewards: Giving What You Can't Keep to Gain What You Can't Lose* (Carol Stream, IL: Tyndale House Publishers, 2003), 7.

3. James W. Fowler, *Stages of Faith: The Psychology of Human Development and the Quest for Meaning* (New York: HarperCollins, 1981).

4. P. H. McNamara, "What People Give Indicates Their Spiritual Health," in *More Than Money: Portraits of Transformative Stewardship* (Bethesda, Md.: The Alban Institute, 1999).

5. Chart adapted from Wesley K. Willmer, *God & Your Stuff* (Colorado Springs, CO: NavPress, 2002), 44–45.

6. Ruth Haley Barton, *Life Together in Christ: The Vital Link Between Your Possessions and Your Soul* (Downers Grove, IL: InterVarsity Press, 2014), 13. Italics hers.

7. Barna Research Group, *The Generosity Gap: How Christians' Perceptions and Practices of Giving Are Changing—and What It Means for the Church* (Ventura, CA: Barna Group, 2017), 23.

8. David Kinnaman and Gabe Lyons, *Good Faith: Being a Christian When Society Thinks You're Irrelevant and Extreme* (Grand Rapids: Baker Books, 2016), 134.

**Chapter Five**

1. Philo of Alexandria, *On Joseph*, 144.    Cf. Bruce Longenecker, *Remember the Poor* (Grand Rapids: Eerdmans, 2010), 111.

2. Thomas Traherne, *Centuries of Meditation* (New York: Cosmo Classics, 2007), 1.7.

3. Ibid.

4. Walter Brueggemann, *Money and Possessions,* part of the series *Interpretation: Resources for the Use of Scripture in the Church* (Louisville, KY: Westminster John Knox Press, 2016), 8.

5. Craig L. Blomberg, *Neither Poverty nor Riches: A Biblical Theology of Material Possessions* (Grand Rapids: Eerdmans, 1999), 247.

6. Alan Barnhart, "God Owns Our Business," https://generousgiving.org/media/videos/alan-barnhart-god-owns-our-business.

7. A. W. Tozer in "The Transmutation of Wealth" in The Alliance Witness (October 8, 1958).

8. Chapter 2 of James K. A. Smith, *You Are What You Love,* 27–56.

9. Francis Schaeffer, *How Should We Then Live?* (Wheaton: Crossway, 2005) 256.

10. Eusebius, *The Church History,* trans. Paul L. Meier (Grand Rapids: Kregel, 2007), 293.

11. Ibid.

## Chapter Six

1. Randy Alcorn, *The Treasure Principle: Unlocking the Secret of Joyful Giving* (Sisters, OR: Multnomah, 2001), 46–47.

2. These are some of the major roadblocks used in the presentation, "What Does It Look Like to Inspire Biblically Grounded Generosity" at the *Inspire Giving Conference* on April 12, 2018.

3. Louise Story, "Anywhere the Eye Can See, It's Likely to See an Ad," *New York Times*, 1/15/07. https://www.nytimes.com/2007/01/15/business/media/15every where.html. Only half the 4,100 people surveyed thought that advertising was out of control.

4. Monroe Friedman, "Are Americans Becoming More Materialistic? A Look at Changes in Expressions of Materialism in the Popular Literature of the Post-World War II Era," *Advances in Consumer Research* volume 12, eds. Elizabeth C. Hirschman and Morris B. Holbrook (Provo, UT: Association for Consumer Research, 1985), 385–387. http://www.acrwebsite.org/search/view-conference -proceedings.aspx?Id=6420

5. Ipsos MORI Thinks, "Millennial: Myths and Realities," 2017, 38–39. https://www .ipsos.com/sites/default/files/2017-05/ipsos-mori-millennial-myths-realities -full-report.pdf

6. See Wesley K. Willmer, "The Shifting Motivations for Giving and Asking: Where Have We Come From, and Where Are We Going?" in *Becoming a Steward Leader: Fundamentally Change the Way You Think, Lead, and Live*, ed. Mark L. Vincent and Joseph Krivickas (San Clemente, CA: Christian Leadership Alliance, 2012), 1–17.

7. Christian Smith and Melinda Lundquist Denton, *Soul Searching: The Religious and Spiritual Lives of American Teenagers* (Oxford, UK: Oxford University Press, 2005).

8. Mark A. Smith, *Secular Faith: How Culture Has Trumped Religion in American Politics* (Chicago: University of Chicago Press, 2015), preface. It should be noted that Smith does not see this as a new phenomenon but an integral part of the relationship of religion and politics in the history of American life.

9. Nonprofit Source, "The Ultimate List of Charitable Giving Statistics for 2018," https://nonprofitssource.com/online-giving-statistics/.

10. James K. A. Smith, *You Are What You Love*, 50.

11. See Mark L. Vincent, "On Being a Steward: Yes It Involves Money" in *Becoming a Steward Leader: Fundamentally Change the Way You Think, Lead, and Live*, ed. Mark L. Vincent and Joseph Krivickas (San Clemente, CA: Christian Leadership Alliance, 2012), 21–24.

12. John Stott, *The Radical Disciple: Some Neglected Aspects of Our Calling* (Downers Grove, IL: InterVarsity Press, 2010), 20.

13. Barna Research Group, *The Generosity Gap: How Christians' Perceptions and Practices of Giving Are Changing - and What It Means for the Church* (Barna Group, 2017).

14. From a personal interview. Used by permission.

15. R. Scott Rodin, "The Temptation to be Spectacular." Blog post at www.thestewards journey.com, 3/5/2019.

16. Neil Postman, *Amusing Ourselves to Death: Public Discourse in the Age of Show Business*, 20th Anniversary Edition (New York: Penguin Books, 2006), 128.

17. Robert Wuthnow, *God and Mammon in America* (New York, MacMillan, 1994), 2–3.

18. Gary G. Hoag, "John Reid: Refocus" on *Generosity Monk* blog, 3/24/2019.

19. *The Didache* in *The Apostolic Fathers: Greek Texts and English Translations, Third Edition.* trans. Michael W. Holmes (Grand Rapids: Baker Academic, 2007), 345.

20. See Wesley K. Willmer, "What Does It Look Like to Inspire Biblically Grounded Generosity" at the *Inspire Giving Conference* on April 12, 2018.

21. Craig L. Blomberg, "God and Money: A Biblical Theology of Possessions" in *Revolution in Generosity: Transforming Stewards to Be Rich Towards God*, ed. Wesley K. Willmer (Chicago: Moody Publishers, 2008), 45.

22. Personal interview, used by permission.

23. For a Christ-centered approach to fundraising, see Gary Hoag, R. Scott Rodin, and Wesley K. Willmer, *The Choice: The Christ-Centered Pursuit of Kingdom Outcomes* (EFCA Press, 2014).

## Chapter Seven

1. Ron Blue with Jeremy White in *Splitting Heirs* (Chicago: Northfield, 2004), 102–103.

2. Gary G. Hoag, *Wealth in Ancient Ephesus and the First Letter to Timothy: Fresh Insights from* Ephesiaca *by Xenophon of Ephesus* (Winona, IN: Eisenbrauns, 2015), 220.

3. St. Basil the Great, *On Social Justice,* trans. C. Paul Schroeder (Crestwood, NY: St. Vladimir's Seminary Press, 2009), 97–98.

4. Randy Alcorn in *The Treasure Principle: Unlocking the Secret of Joyful Giving* (Sisters, OR: Multnomah, 2001), 18.

5. St. Basil the Great, *On Social Justice,* 63, 57.

6. R. T. France, *The Gospel of Matthew* (NICNT; Grand Rapids: Eerdmans, 2007), 748–49.

7. Keith Krell, "The Judgement Seat of Christ." Used at Fourth Memorial Church in Spokane, Washington.

8. C. S. Lewis, *The Weight of Glory* (San Francisco: HarperCollins, 2001), 25–26.

9. This exegesis is drawn from Jean Luc-Marion's excellent interpretation in *God without Being: Hors-Texte, Second Edition*, trans. Thomas A. Carlson (Chicago: University of Chicago Press, 2012), 95–101.

### Chapter Eight

1. Karl Barth, *Church Dogmatics IV/3.2*, trans. G. W. Bromiley, ed. G. W. Bromiley and T. F. Torrance (Peabody, MS: Hendrickson Pub., 2010), 779.

2. From a personal interview, used by permission.

3. *Revolution in Generosity*, ed. Wesley K. Willmer (Chicago: Moody Publishers, 2008), 246-247.

4. See Chip Ingram, *The Genius of Generosity* (Generous Church, 2011).

5. Wesley K. Willmer, "5 Step Process to Kingdom-Focused Excellence" in *Outcomes*, Fall 2015, 26.

6. Chris Willard and Jim Sheppard, *Contagious Generosity: Creating a Culture of Giving in Your Church* (Grand Rapids, Zondervan, 2012), 29.

7. From a personal interview. Used by permission.

8. Roger Lam, *Lost and Found: Money vs. Riches* (Nashville, TN: Elm Hill, 2018), 29.

9. Ibid. Capitalization in original.

10. Barna Research Group, "How Technology Is Changing Millennial Faith," 2003, https://www.barna.com/research/how-technology-is-changing-millennial -faith/.

11. John Wesley, *A Plain Account of Christian Perfection*, 11:5. Accessed at https:// www.worldinvisible.com/library/wesley/8317/831711.htm.

### Chapter Nine

1. Charles Haddon Spurgeon as recounted by David Jeremiah, *Turning Points: Finding Moments of Refuge in the Presence of God* (Nashville: Thomas Nelson, 2006), 184.

2. R. Scott Rodin, "A Vision for the Generous Life" in *Christ-Centered Generosity: Global Perspectives on the Biblical Call to a Generous Life*, ed. R. Scott Rodin (Colbert, WA: Kingdom Life Publishing, 2015), 8.

3. From an unpublished testimonial. Used by permission.

4. From a personal interview. Used by permission.

5. From a personal interview. Used by permission.

6. Johnson Oatman, "Count Your Blessings," accessed at https://hymnary.org/text/ when_upon_lifes_billows_you_are_tempest.

7. Karl Barth, *Church Dogmatics* IV/3.2, ed. G. W. Bromiley and T. F. Torrance, trans. G. W. Bromiley (Edinburgh: T. & T. Clark, 1962), 779.

8. Maximus of Turin, from Sermon 71: "On Fasting and Almsgiving," in *The Sermons of St. Maximus of Turin*, trans. Boniface Ramsey, OP (New York: Newman Press, 1989), 175.

9. Barna Research Group, *The Generosity Gap*, 18.

10. From a personal interview. Used by permission.

11. Kyle David Bennet, *Practices of Love: Spiritual Disciplines for the Life of the World* (Grand Rapids, MI: Brazos Press, 2017), 22–23.    Italics his.

## Conclusion

1. Helen H. Lemmel, "Turn Your Eyes Upon Jesus," hymnal.net.

# ACKNOWLEDGEMENTS

O
ver the years, God has worked through many wonderful people to shape my life and thinking. This book is the result of the influence of many people, and I am grateful to each person, named and unnamed, that I have had the privilege to affiliate and interact with in many different settings.

The following friends and colleagues were willing to review early copies of the work to provide direction and suggestions for improvement: Dan Busby, Tami Heim, Gary Hoag, Keith Krell, Rick Rood, John Pearson, and Sid Yeoman. In addition, many friends around the country provided dialogue over the years that enhanced the work. Some of those included: Tim Connor, Todd Harper, Rich Haynie, Nathan Jones, Brian Kluth, Jay Link, Lee Maxwell, Chris McDaniel, Scott Rodin, Mark Vincent, and others that were interviewed and allowed their stories to be used.

Micah Hogan was a tremendous partner as a researcher and writer that served with me throughout this project. He came alongside with his biblical, theological, and practical perspective as a millennial to keep this effort moving with his energy, ideas, competence, and expertise. The end product would not have been what it is without his capable involvement.

A special thanks to God for my mother, Diantha S. Willmer, who throughout the years has been an encourager to me and now, as she approaches the century mark of life, she is still asking about my writing projects.

Finally I thank God for my wife of almost fifty years, Sharon, and for our adult children, Stephen Paul, Anna Kristell, and Jonathan Brian and his wife, Lindsay—all of whom God has used to shape my life. In addition, God has blessed us with seven grandchildren: Addie, Amy, Emma, Gwyneth, Nehemiah, Titus, and Wesley.

It is my earnest prayer that God will use this book to change lives to further His eternal Kingdom through a better understanding of our stuff, soul, and being rich toward God as it helps fulfill the Great Commission.

—Wesley K. Willmer

# ABOUT THE AUTHORS

WESLEY K. WILLMER, Ph.D., CCNL, has served with or for various Christian ministries for five decades and is known as a pioneer among Christian leaders in encouraging Christians to follow God's plan for money, giving, and asking. In 1987, he initiated and directed the national conference "Funding the Christian Challenge," which attracted nationwide media attention in such publications as *Christianity Today, U.S. News & World Report, Fund Raising Management,* and the *Washington Post.*

Wes has initiated and directed more than $1 million in research grants to study nonprofit practices, and he has been the author, coauthor, editor, or editor-in-chief of over twenty-three books and many professional journal articles and publications. Selected book titles include: *The Prospering Parachurch* (Jossey-Bass), *God and Your Stuff* (NavPress), *Revolution in Generosity* (Moody Press), *The Choice* (ECFAPress), and *The Council* (ECFAPress). *Fund Raising Management* magazine selected him to write on the future of funding religion for its twenty-fifth anniversary issue.

He has held executive leadership positions at Biola University, the Evangelical Council for Financial Accountability (ECFA), Far East Broadcasting Company (FEBC), Mission Increase Foundation, Prison Fellowship Ministries, Roberts Wesleyan College, Seattle Pacific University, and Wheaton College (IL), and he was a faculty member at each of these educational institutions. His board involvement includes chair of the board of the Christian Stewardship

Association (CSA), vice chair of the Evangelical Council for Financial Accountability (ECFA) board, founding board member and executive committee member of the Christian Leadership Alliance (CLA), CASE International Journal of Educational Advancement, and consultant to other boards.

In 1986, the Council for Advancement and Support of Education (CASE) selected Willmer from among its 14,000 individual members to receive its annual award for significant contributions in research and writing. In 1999, the Christian Stewardship Association honored him as the Outstanding Stewardship Professional. In 2005, the Biola University Torrey Honors Institute selected him as a perpetual member. Seattle Pacific University selected him in 2010 as one of 100 distinguished "alumni of a growing vision" out of the more than 40,000 alumni. And in 2016, the Seattle Pacific University Centurions honored him with the Roy Swanstrom Distinguished Centurion Award.

MICAH HOGAN is a freelance researcher and writer pursuing his Master of Divinity at Nashotah House Theological Seminary and is the theology editor at *The PQ Review*. In 2019, he graduated from the Torrey Honors Institute of Biola University (La Mirada, CA) with a BA in biblical and theological studies. He was inducted into the Torrey Honors Institute's Order of Peter and Paul for academic excellence and received the G. Campbell Morgan Award for continued pursuit and articulation of God's truth. He has studied abroad in Rome, Italy, and Oxford, England.